GW00838689

ISBN: 978-1-5272-3808-4

1

A little info about my beginnings

I was born at the beginning of 1951 in Withington Hospital, Manchester ... Just 22 weeks into me Mum's pregnancy with me and weighed in at just 2lb ... I was a very weak and sickly child and spent the first four years and more of my life in and out of hospital ...

The early years of me childhood that I can remember, were full of derelict empty buildings .... Houses, shops and old factories set between Stretford Road and City Road .... And this was home as it was all we knew but it was our world .... This was a lovely place to live as us kids didn't realise we lived in slums ... To us the old wrecked buildings were our castles, ranches and jungles we had seen at the Saturday matinees at the York picture house ...

And yeah, we had lots of good friends and family who lived close by and were always ready to just have fun ... On good days me Dad would take me to the Barracks Park with me older sister Pam, while me Mum watched the younger siblings ...

Then on a few occasions at weekends me Dad would take me to Alexandra Park lake with him where he would try his best to sail the various types of boats and wooden ships he had made in our back yard after coming home from work over the hot summer months, on the lake in the park ... Sadly though none of his boats, to my memory anyway, ever seemed to float or sail very well at all ..... Me poor old Dad

Just after the Christmas of 1957, but before the New Year 1958, we, the family, moved to our new home in Woodhouse Park in Wythenshawe, near Manchester Airport, that was known as Ringway Airport back when I was a nipper, where most of my adventures and memories were made ...

This new house seemed to me like a huge castle with giant rooms and it even had a indoor toilet and a proper bath with taps ... Wow ... magic or what? ... And the large gardens back and front of the house ... Oh yes! ... This was a great new world to start my new adventures.

CONTENTS

1

<u>My stories start in Hulme, Manchester</u>

Some of the earliest memories I have of growing up in Manchester are the ones of the days me late Dad, in the early 1950's in Hulme, would take me around the old bombed out buildings that were remnants left over from the heavy bombing of Manchester and Salford during the second world war ... Where we would collect all shapes, types and sizes of wood ...

Me Dad would cut the timbers up into easy to handle sizes, then stack the timber up and tie them down onto the four wheeled bogey that he had made ... Then take the timber home to burn on our fire in the house ... Where we lived on Mowbray Street ...

The fire was where most things revolved around as it was where me Mam would cook the food, when we had food to cook that is, heat the water for bathing, washing clothes and making brews ... And dry the washing and heat up the house ...

There was no toilet in the house nor built in bath, just a tin bath and no taps ... We got us water from a green steel pump in the yard ... And the only light in the house was a gas light that was situated on the wall about 5 feet from the floor and above us fire place ..... The problem was this light, being gas, whenever we had a good roaring fire going the heat from the fire would make the gas light go out ... Oh the joys of gas lights ...

The only furniture we had was a green kitchen cabinet in our living room and two Wilson's wooden beer crates with a plank across them as a bench ... And a steel wash bin and a mangle in the kitchen ...

And upstairs a double bed for us Mam and Dad to sleep in and a wooden tea chest they kept their clothes in to stop the mice from chewing their clothes ... and a single bed for me and me elder sister Pam, which we shared ...

I remember me Dad would come in from work each night, come up to me and our Pam's room with a candle in a brass candle holder, kneel down at the side of us bed and say prayers ... Then kiss both me and our Pam on us foreheads saying, "May God bless you and keep you safe." ... Then leave our room and go back downstairs ...

Back then everyone we knew in Hulme lived under the same harsh conditions ... Yet they all helped each other out as best they could and shared what they had, no one was richer or poorer than their neighbour ... Strange I know, but that's how I remember it ...... A great loving community spirit .... Even when us kids played out there was always at least two eagle eyed old ladies watching over us so no harm could befall us kids ...

I have very fond memories of those early years of my life though they were very hard times ... I know I was blessed because I heard many a tale of other families in other areas having things much worse than we had .... At least me Dad and most of the other local men had jobs in our neck of the woods ....

Me Dad was the eldest of six brothers and just days before I was born his Dad had died leaving his Mum, my Gran, with the task of raising these five sons on her own ...

But me Dad made arrangements with his Mum that he would give her all the help he could and would pay the rent for her ... But the older of the other siblings would have to find some kind of part time work after school and at weekends ...

But disaster struck the family again ... Me Dad's next eldest brother down, Kevin, was crushed by a truck on Chester Road on his way home from school and lost both his legs due to the accident ... He was just twelve years old at the time of this life changing accident .... And poor Kevin spent so many, many years of his life in and out of hospitals ...

But eventually Kevin made it through due to his strengh of character ... and the very tight knit family he belonged too ...

Hope this information has given you a taste of where my roots took hold and my life's adventures began .... which I now share with you.

2

<u>My first seaside holiday</u>

Feeling so sad yet nostalgic as I share with you this very precious memory of me at the young tender age of five .... This memory I share with you is one of me Ninny Emma, me Granddad Alf and me Uncle Ray ...

This story begins on the day when they took me on holiday to Morecambe ... The journey on the train as I remember seemed to take a lifetime to get there once we left the railway station in Manchester ... I had never been on a train nor heard them start up close up ... The jerk and thunderous roar as the engine fired up and started to roll ... Wow! ...

As we pulled out of the station and the hooter on the train hooted very loudly and the rumbling in me chest from the train now in motion was amazing though scary too ... As we left our back to back homes and crofts behind ... We soon passed all the old houses, mills and factories and were now out in the open countryside and out of the city ...

That in itself was a very strange experience as I had

never seen such large green frields, hedge rows and farm animals ... I had been told about horses, cows, sheep, pigs, geese and chickens but never had I seen live ones ... So you can imagine how strange these sights were for me ... It was just amazing ...

As we travelled on and on me Granddad Alf told me stories of when he was a boy and just like me, had seen live farm animals for the first time too .... And how the farmers grew crops like potatoes, cabbages and so on .....

I must have fallen asleep as my next memory is of us leaving the train station in Morecambe and getting on a coach to the camp site where we would live for the next week in a thing called a caravan home ... Well after getting the keys and going into the caravan it was lovely ... Lots of seats, a cooker and a radio to keep us entertained ... After unpacking, Ninny and Uncle Ray went to the camp chippy and got us all fish and chips for us supper ....

My next memory must have been the next day as it was a bright, hot, sunny day and we were all walking along the beach collecting shells for Ninny and when we had a bag full we built sand castles and had a picnic on the beach ... Then off back to the caravan ....

The next day we all walked around looking in the shops getting gifts and some shopping ... Then back to the caravan to have an early supper and early night in bed as in the morning Granddad said we were off across the sea to the Isle of Man ....

The next morning, true to his word, we all boarded a ship and across the sea we went to the Isle of Man ... Where we all started to go up this never ending staircase that led to the top of a place called Bradda Head .... Well me poor old Ninny just couldn't make it all the way up so we sat down on a rock whilst Granddad and Uncle Ray climbed to the top and we waited for them to return ...

Whilst we were waiting a young couple passed us and Ninny said, "I have a camera. Will you please take a photo of me and me Grandson?" ... Which they did and then they carried on up the steps ...

Granddad and Uncle Ray returned so down the steps we went to the bottom where I recall going into a cafe and having a drink and a pie ...

The next memory I have of the day was going inside a huge cave next to the sea and going to see this giant red wheel ...

Little did I know at the time that me Grandparents would not be around much longer ... I had spent most of me early years before this holiday in and out of Withington Hospital as I was born just 22 weeks into me Mum's pregnancy with me and only weighed 2lb at birth and had bronchial pneumonia ...

And during my younger days I developed several serious illnesses leading up to this holiday ... The only holiday I would ever get to have with them .... But these early years and the memories they have left me will remain with me forever ...

Not long after we returned to Manchester me Ninny Emma became ill and about a year later became bed bound and very poorly with diabetes and just seemed to always be asleep when me Mam and Dad would take us kids to visit her, me Granddad and Uncle Ray ...

Between the Christmas of 1957 and the New Year of 1958 me Mam and Dad moved with us four kids, me older sister Pam, me, me younger brother Steve and me younger sister Kim, out of our slum clearance house in Hulme to a lovely newly built big house with large gardens in Wythenshawe .... It was like moving to heaven .... So much countryside, open spaces and a new school ... Bedroom of me own, electric lights now, not a gas light and a stove to cook on and not a fire .... We even had a real bath not a tin one and an inside toilet ... Brilliant eh? ...

Yeah but I had left all me mates, me grandparents, me dens, crofts and all the people, streets, places and faces that I knew, so it was really hard and sad at first ...

And I never got to see me Ninny Emma alive again as she passed away just over a year after we moved out of Hulme into our new house in Wythenshawe ... The last time I saw me Ninny Emma was on the day of her funeral ... She was lay in her coffin in me Granddad's front room parlour ....

And there were some haunting words the undertaker said to me Granddad that I'll never forget which were, ... "The lady has some very expensive rings on her fingers and we can't just pull them off ... But if you want them we have finger cutters ... One quick snip and you'll have your rings." .... "That's my wife!" Yelled me Granddad and grabbed the undertaker by the scruff of his neck ...

Me Dad grabbed me and took me out of the parlour rather sharpish and took me into the living room down the hall way ... So I never saw or heard anything else said ...

Me next recollection is being at me lovely Ninny's graveside in Southern Cemetery as they lowered her coffin down into her grave ... I still miss me Ninny Emma so very much even to this day over sixty years later.

3

<u>Me, me Dad and his boats</u>

Here's another little story I wish to share with you ... This one is from when I was about three to four years old ....

Me late Dad had a fascination with model making, especially model boats .... So whatever time he had spare, you'd find him in the back yard in Hulme in Manchester cutting, chiselling, sanding and glueing bits of thin pieces of wood together and making what would look like the old fashioned Spanish galleons ... They looked brilliant ...

Then me Dad would get some pieces of dowelling and hanky sized cotton pieces for making the sails with ...

Then wrap it all up in a bag, put the main ship under his arm and shout in the house to me Mam, ... "Right then Babs." ... That was me Mam's name .... "I'm off now with me boy, and I'll teach him about sailing model ships on the lakes." ...

And off he'd take me to Alexandra Park in Moss Side

to the lake ...

Where he would put all the ship's parts together, place the ship in the water with the wind behind us and wait for the wind to come and blow into the sails of me Dad's lovely little ship to blow it to the other side of the lake ....

Yeah! ... Er, no ... cos every time, the ships me lovely Dad had made only travelled out from the bank a few feet when disaster always struck ...

Either the ship would just roll over on its side or the ship would just simply sink ... Me Dad would wade in and get the ship back, while muttering under his breath words I didn't understand at the time ...

But then the good part ... Me Dad would then take me to the water lion fountain to get a drink of water .... Then, yippee! ... He would take me to get an ice cream from the ice cream parlour ... um um um ... lovely ...

Then we'd have the long walk of failure home with our heads bowed low over another ship that failed to work ... Me poor old Dad never did manage to get one of those ships to work right ...

But what great memories I have of those long hot summer days of trying them model boats out ... And I hoped to learn things from our, well me Dad's failures ....

Me Dad also made a couple of bogeys that we thought were very good, they had what he called a stick brake that worked like this ... As you pulled the top part of the stick towards you, the bottom part of the stick would drag on the floor and slow you down ... Great idea eh? ha ha ha ...

That was me Dad's way, trying things out ... And then he put an old car lamp on the front of the bogey that was connected to a car battery behind the seat so the bogey had a light at the front ... Not that I ever went out on one in the dark ...

I really loved those bygone days spent with the best man I have ever known ...

Me lovely Dad was only 55 years old when he passed away, and he was me best friend ... I love and miss him so very much.

4

<u>Our last Bonfire Night in Hulme</u>

Here's a memory I think we can all share and you can throw in your two pence of memories with mine too eh? ...

Round about the beginning of October time each year back in the day .... Most of us kids would get together with us local gangs and have a truce ..... Bet you remember that don't you? .....Well just in case you don't remember before I carry on I'll give you a clue ....

Let's go kids ... Find a good large croft and clear it up and put some bricks that we would find in to a neat pile at the side of the croft .....

After clearing and sorting out the croft you would put a couple of mates by the bricks to stand guard ... Usually the biggest lads out of the gangs ..... Bet the grey matter's warming up now eh? ...... We're nearly there, come on .....

Then we would all go out all over the place and go in

all the derelict buildings and even the old fenced off areas ... And yeah you got it now eh? ... Ha ha ha ...We would start collecting as much bungy wood as we could carry .... or stack our bogeys with as much as they could take ... And take it all back to our cleared up croft and start stacking it up in size order piles ....

Well, we all had in each area a giant pile of wood that was getting bigger and bigger as each night we collected wood after school and at weekends too ... Then we would collect even more so by the time the big night came, it, the wood that is, looked like it reached right up to the sky ....

Especially this year as there were so many abandoned and derelict properties around due to the Hulme slum clearance programme ... This made our stacks of wood well, to be honest, huge ....What was left of all the local gangs of kids in our part of Hulme had joined together this year and made the biggest stacks of wood that even the adults could recall and they had not seen the likes of before ....

Then on the big night the adults came along with home made treacle toffee, home made parkin cake ...

toffee apples and a few fireworks ...

And some men came, bringing with them on the back of a horse and cart a couple of old pianos that some adults later played ... And all the adults sang along to the tunes being played on the pianos ...Whilst our mountain of a bonfire burned higher and higher ....

But later on when the flames finally died down a bit us kids made squares with some bricks right up against the hot cinders, put some spuds in and put a couple more bricks on top as a roof .... Then just waited for us spuds to bake ... Yeah man, brilliant! .... Bet you're remembering those days now and your mouth has begun to water! .... Um um um where's the butter? Whoor yeah! .... Not yet though!...You're gonna need a bit of wood to put your spud on cos they're blumming red hot! ... Now that's better ...

Now get ready to WHOOOOO! WHARRRRRR! ... Cos the adults are setting off the fireworks ... First the Roman candles, then the Catherine wheels, then more ground fireworks and the bangers ...

Whilst the little uns played with the Bengal matches and sparklers .... Whooooooosh would go the first

rocket, followed by another and another, whoor! ...
Yeah! ...

But oh boy! ... How we all stunk of gunpowder and
fire smoke for days after ... And that smog the day
after Bonfire Night ... Yuk! .....

I'll bet there's a good few of you that got the embers
going again the morning after Bonfire Night just to
make a little fire again eh? ....

Hope this last Bonfire Night in Hulme story has
brought back some fond memories for you too ... Stay
safe, warm, healthy, happy and young at heart always.

Who remembers singing, "Light up the sky with
Standard Fireworks." ... As you watched your rockets
fly high into the night sky with your faces lit up by the
light of the bonfire.

5

<u>My last Christmas in old Hulme</u>

Hope you've got some tea and toast in hand ... As I take you down memory lane to the first Christmas I ever recall ...

It was just before we moved to Wythenshawe ... It was a damp, bitterly cold, smoggy Christmas Eve night ... We, me Mam, me Dad, me and me elder sister Pam ... were all huddled round the fire ... Me Dad built up the fire even more with large lumps of coal, and then said to me Mam, ... "Wrap up the kids love. ... We'll go see me Mam" ... Me and our Pam, me elder sister, called her Ninny Ratcliff ...

Anyway, after being wrapped up by me Mam, we headed off out to Ninny Ratcliff's home ... It took us what seemed like forever to get there ...

On the way we walked along the main road, where there was a man walking and carrying a lamp light in front of a bus ... Followed by a man walking behind the bus, also carrying a light, leading a horse pulling a cart with a man sat up front on top smoking a pipe or a cigarette, I think, as every so often his face would light up a reddish orange ...

The cart had what looked like large beer barrells on the back ... I can't say for sure as it was very hard to make things out for sure through the smog ... But these men had seen us through the smog and called out to us, ... "All the very best to you and the kids ... Merry Christmas." ... As they passed us and disappeared in to the smog and night going in the opposite direction from us ....

The next thing I recall is me Mam bumping in to a man who was dimly lit under a gas light with a tiny dog on a piece of string ... And both me Mam and this man said sorry at the same time ... and wished each other a merry Christmas and we were on us way again

I could now hear faint music somewhere out there in the smog and darkness ... and as we carried on walking the music got louder and louder .... Then I could see what looked like a dull cloud of light ... That got brighter as we carried on walking ... Now through the smog I could see a man lit up down one side playing what I now know to be a barrell organ and the light was Paulden's department store just off to our right ...

We crossed the road and went in to the large store ...
Me Mam, me Dad, me and sister Pam ... and me Dad
took us to see Santa ... Yeah man, what a treat! ...
Really excited, whoor! ... I got to see Santa for real! ...
Well, we left the shop and now me Dad had
something wrapped in brown paper and we headed off
to Jackson Street flats to see me Ninny Ratcliff, our
gran ....

The next memory I have of this night is me Dad
coming back to where me Mam and us kids were
stood under a gas lamp next to a pub on a corner ....
And me Dad saying to me Mam, "Sorry love, she still
won't let you in." ... But us Dad said to us Mam, "But
it's ok for me and the kids to go in." .... Me Mam just
said, "It's ok, let her be like that." ...

Then me Dad, just took us, me and our Pam, in to see
our grandma, Ninny Ratcliff ... Who gave us a hug
and said, "Merry Christmas." ...

Then we were back under the gas lamp with me Mam
and headed off home ... I have no memory of the
journey back to our house ... Which was Maple Street,

Hulme, Manchester .....

Just a little side note ... Me younger brother Steve had been born by this point but I don't recall him being with us at all ... But he may have been at me Mam's parents' house, who lived round the corner from where we lived ...

Anyway, we got home into our house, then me Dad stoked the fire up and lit the gas mantle above the fire place while me Mam hung some nappies she had washed over the wooden clothes horse to dry ... Then we all sat huddled up again round the fire and me Dad cooked some chestnuts in a home guard's tin helmet over the fire ...

The next morning, Christmas Day ... Me Mam and Dad took us kids to our Mum's parents' house just around the corner, over on Erskine Street ... Where we were given our Christmas presents and we all had the traditional roast goose dinner ... Then, home made by me Nanna, a great big piece of apple pie, yummy yum yum ...

Then after eating us munch and giving thanks we went down into the cellar that me Granddad had painted all white and bright which made it a nice bright place to play ... Even though it was only lit by a couple of candles sat on two upside down steel bins near to the coal hole ...

We played with our Uncle Ray, me Mam's much younger brother who is only seven years older than me older sister Pam, who is just a year older than me ... We had great fun playing with Ray's new train set, my castle and soldiers and Pam with her two dolls, a pram and doll's feeding set ....

I hope you liked reading about the first Christmas I recall round at me grandparents house ...

I never did find out why me Mam and Ninny Ratcliff, me Dad's Mum didn't get on ... But there again I never dared ask ...

I'll bet you have some top Christmas memories too from your childhood days ... The faces, places, names and toys ... Misty coloured memories we all carry throughout our lives ... What would we all be without our memories I wonder?

6

<u>Finding Smokey the dog</u>

Hello there again and hope you're in fine fettle ... and not feeling too woof .... Now that's an intro to another memory lane story ... Please hop aboard me memory train and take a ride back into the past with me ....

This story I'll start right at the beginning and hope you've all got your brew and butties ready on the arm of your favourite chair .....

One sunny but cold February day I went playing out on me new scooter I had got as a present for Christmas ... You know the sort I mean ... The type where you have to put one foot on the base board and the other down on to the floor and push yourself along

We had only moved into this area, Wythenshawe, a few weeks earlier from Hulme due to the slum clearance of Hulme at the time ...

Well I scooted down to our local shops, growling like a motorbike round the shops I went .... Yeah baby top stuff! ... eee bar gum I can see meself now ... Brum!

Brum! .... Then down the road I was off again ... On the pavement though, I ain't stupid you know, just daft ... ha ha ha .... From the Cornishman shops on me way now to the Portway shops ....

Just passed the school, Moss Nook, on Portway, I met two pals I had made friends with just after moving into our new house ... Tommy .... and Billy ... who had got fishing rods for their Christmas presents and were on their way to a small pond that was at the side of the school, just behind the caretaker's house on Portway ...

So I asked, "Can I come with you? Will you show me how you catch fish then?" ... "Yeah." they said ... So off we went ... It wasn't far to get to the little pond, just about fifty yards ..... Now then, here's where you're gonna say ore awe no ......

Cos just as we got to the water's edge I saw there was a couple of rubbish sacks, hessian types ... You know, the older readers will remember them, like the GPO used to use ... with bits of rubbish in them ... Before me friends had chance to start fishing ... one of the bags started to tremble and shake, then go still again, then tremble, then go still ...

Well, while the lads set up their rods to start fishing, me, being the nosey one, untied the bag that was trembling to find inside what looked like wet furry black puddings ... but one of the puddings was steaming .... Well, steam coming off it and it was moving a bit ... So I pulled all these furry things out of the bag and laid them on the bank at the pond's edge ... 'cept the one that was moving ...

I wiped away from what I thought was its face bits of what looked like horse hair and bits of fluff .... Then I could see a little black nose, little black ears and little white blue eyes .... and a little mouth ... I think you know what is was? ... Arh yeah, I'll tell you in a minute ...

The other black balls of fur were freezing and even I knew, as a young kid, whatever animals these had been, they were sadly now dead ...

So this one that was alive I stuck it down me top though it was wet, dirty and freezing ... So I told Tommy and Billy what I had and told them I was gonna take it home to me Dad ....

They said, "Ya Mam will leather you, ... you messed

ya new Christmas clothes up." ... I said, "Yeah I know, but I need to get home with this wet furry thing ... to see if me Dad can fix it" ... So off I went ... struggling trying to get home with me scooter as this thing kept falling out the bottom of me top

Anyway I finally got home, shouted me Dad, who when he saw it took it off me and dried and cleaned it up properly .... While I'm stood there mouth wide open ... like you could get a sideboard in there .... When me Dad said, "You done good son ... it's a little boy puppy .... Someone must have dumped them in the pond." ....

He then went into the kitchen, got a stera milk bottle, mixed up some national dried baby milk, put it in the stera bottle and put a teat on it and tried to feed the puppy ... but the teat was too big ...

The poor little puppy couldn't fit it in his mouth ... So me Dad got and used an eye dropper ... filled it with the milk and fed the puppy ... He kept on having to re-fill it though ...

Well me Dad and me over the next few weeks worked hard looking after that little chap ... Weened him onto meat, house trained him .... And we named him Smokey as he steamed so much on the day I found him ... Smokey, me dog lived and was me bestest pal for over seventeen years ... And had joined me on so many of me childhood adventures ....

Towards the end Smokey suffered a stroke which affected his ability to walk then he had a heart attack ... Me Dad took him to the vets in Gatley where me heart was broken as he passed away at the vets and never would be me companion again

Bet you have some tales to tell of your first dog and best friend eh? .... Hope you liked this memory I have shared with you, and have enjoyed this, another trip down memory lane.

7

<u>Our first big day in the countryside</u>

The summer of 1958 was the first summer we spent in the fields and woods of Wythenshawe after moving here from Hulme in late December 1957 ...

Well being kids, me and our Pam, me elder sister, didn't take too long to make friends and go exploring in the local fields and woodlands ...

We had moved here from the slums and crofts of Hulme, Manchester ... So being amongst all this countryside was a dream come true ....

Well now our first major trip out took us to a place the other kids locally told us was called Castle Mills ... Which was a beautiful place with fields, woods and a lovely clear water river called the River Bollin ... So on us way we went ...

Over the first field we called the Farmer's field, turned right down Ringway Road, passed the old and flooded air raid shelters on us right, then over the field with a little pond called Keeper's field ... Then walked by the

Romper pub and the tiny Ringway Church ... Then passed Sunbank Farm and into Castle Mills Woods and down Pigley Steps, that are cut into the hill side ... to the main Bollin field ....

We had taken us some jam butties and some bottles of water and it was a lovely hot summer's day ... So it wasn't too long before we were having us a paddle in the shallow parts of the River Bollin and during which time we waded across to a pebble island where we planned a game of cowboys and Indians ...

Across the other side of the field, away from the River Bollin, and the field we were in, was a wood called Sunbank Wood ....

There a few of the kids made a camp for the Indians and on the island in the river would be the pretend cavalry fort ... Then with Dave Tate doing the directing and commentating the game commenced ... So off we ran, across the field slapping our hips thinking our legs were horses ....

And we attacked each others little camps, shouting "Peeyang peeyang ... You're dead." ... And "Whoosh ping" was the arrow sound the Indians made with their pretend arrows ... and shouted at the cowboys "Got ya, you're dead." ... Bet you're remembering doing this as a kid back in your childhood eh? Ha ha ha ... After we had attacked each others camps a couple of times a winner was declared and the game was over ...

Then we shared out us jam butties and water we had left while sitting on the grass in the shade of the trees near to Pigley Steps before making our long trek home through Sunbank Woods, across the fields, then passed the Romper and then the airport, then over the Farmer's field at the back of Ravenscar Crescent, passed the flats, down the hill and home at last where we all separated and went to our own homes ...

So we went in our houses and told us Mams and Dads of our little adventure, but great day out down by the River Bollin at Castle Mills with our new found mates we had made since moving to Wythenshawe ....

That day there was a good little gang of us kids ... There was Dave and Ayo Tate, John Benn, Rob Jones, Tony Leo, Steve Chrich, Noel Woods, Ruth Dumph, our Pam, Eddy Dunn, Chris Collins, Barry Greenwood, Otto Fido and some other kids I don't remember the names of ...

Do you remember your old pals from way back? ... Bet you remember a lot of them ... I can still remember those long hot summer days of our childhood innocence ... And our first of many adventures around Castle Mills, Styal Woods and the good old River Bollin ... Though they're drifting away these days, in the mists of time ...

We even found a large overgrown pond that was at the edge of the woods by the bridal path and at the side of the breather shaft of the old tin mine that ran beneath the hill ... The pond was filled with rubbish left over from the Second World War and the training equipment dumped by the parachutists who had trained at Manchester Airport in the years gone by in and around Sunbank Woods ...

We cleaned out the old pond the best we could and stocked it with fish we had caught in the local ponds ... Over the next few years it was a good little place to go fishing, playing, camping and making top dens ...

Sadly the Kids these days have much different ways

of having fun ... But I prefer the old ways ... Out and about in the muck making dens, climbing trees and just having a great imagination as a way of having fun with the simplest of things ....

The laughter of children filling the air along with the sounds of song birds was beautiful ... Sadly now those sounds have just drifted away into the foggy mists of time and so called progress ....

But for me it's time now to wave me old Stetson, slap me hips and ride out into the sunset with my fading memories ... And say till the next time, I'll see ya pal .... We'll catch up next time ......

8

<u>The Corral tree house</u>

Howdy me cowfolk ... I'm just drifting back again down me good old misty memory lane ...

This memory starts with our Colin, Me Dad's youngest brother ... Who is only three years older than I am and had called down from Moss Side where he lived to play with me and me mates .... and show off his new toy, a hoola hoop ...

Well our Colin was running down the road with this hoola hoop and stick, whipping the hoola hoop with his stick to make it go faster ... With me and me mate Ayo following, slapping the living daylights out of us hips thinking our legs were horses as we did back then and trying us best to keep up with our Colin ...

When a shout rang out from another mate named Oggy from across the road asking, ... "And where are you lot off to then?" ... Our Colin yelled back, ... "We're off to the Corral mate ... Ya wanna come with us?" .... Oggy shouted, "Hang on then and I'll ask me Mam if I can go with you." ... So Colin stopped and we pulled back our reigns and waited to see if Oggy would be allowed to come with us ...

Well folks, his Mam said, "Yeah but don't be late." ... So off we went again, our Colin leading the way with his hoola hoop and stick and us three troopers running, slapping our hips behind trying us best to keep up with him ...

Well our Colin led us to the gate on Woodhouse Lane which we climbed over to enter the corral field, then walked down the path to the swamp area about a hundred yards across the field ... Then we all sat down to rest on a bit of a raised bank at the side of the swamp next to an old Anderson air raid shelter ... and started to get us breath back ....

There were several trees surrounding the swamp and a plank that led across the swamp to a small island with a large oak tree in the middle of the island and a few bushes around the edges ...

Oggy blurted out, "What the heck have we come here for then Colin? ... Well, we had never heard anyone question our Colin like this before and were expecting a fight to break out ...

But our Colin calmly walked over to the base of the big old oak tree and just leaned his hoola hoop against it, reached up his hand into the branches and pulled out a rope with a piece of wood tied to it ...

"Uh?" we all grunted, "What's that, a swing?" .... Our Colin said, "You should know what it is." ... Eerr yeah ... Ayo said, "A rope with a few knots in it and a piece of wood tied to the end?" .... "Nope", our Colin said, "You're all idiots ... look up." ... So slowly we all raised up our eyes and looked into the tree canopy ....

And guess what we saw? ... Yup, a huge, well ... a pretty big tree house .... "Whoooorrrr!" we all said, "Whose is that and who built it?" ... Colin said, "It's ours .... Me and our Baz have spent the last few weekends coming down to build it." .... "Naaaaarrrr" we said, "How come you didn't call for us to help you then?" ...

Well Baz is the next eldest up from Colin in age ... And is another of my Dad's younger brothers ... This is getting hard to explain, ... but I hope you're following so far ...

Baz was a girl's lad and loved to be around girls and

show off and this tree house was a place he could bring his new girlfriends without me Gran beating the heck out of him ...

Back to the story ... Our Colin said, "Come on then let's go up and have a mooch eh lads?" .... So we all climbed up into the tree house ... and it was the best tree house we had ever seen .... There were bottles of water, and an old primus stove up there with a kettle, a tea pot, three cups, tea, cocoa, sugar, and National dried powdered milk to make brews with ... Wow this is the life eh? ...

So we just sat up there amazed and chatting and making plans about maybe sleeping over night up in the tree house if our Mams would let us ....

Then Colin said, "C'mon let's go down and make a swing and a better bridge over the swamp to the island." .... There was a long piece of rope left over in the tree house so we climbed down out of the tree house, threw the rope over a thick branch of the oak tree near the entrance to the tree house and tied it up ... So now we had us a swing as well as a tree house ... Yeah, great stuff, yippee! ....

Now we were all taking it in turns swinging on our new swing out over the plank bridge and mud of the swamp ... Brilliant! ... And the laughter of children having fun must have rung out all over the place ...

But suddenly Oggy clapped his hands and said, "Shush everyone! Somebody's coming across the Corral field heading this way!" ... So we all quickly climbed back up into the tree house to hide .... Well it didn't take long before Our Colin said, "It's our Baz ... and it looks like he's brought his latest girlfriend! Oh shiiiiiit! ... I don't even know this one's name!"....

Then Baz was now at the base of the tree with his girlfriend ... and shouted out, "Who's up there then?" ... Our Colin shouted back, "It's me Col, Tony, Ayo and Oggy" ... Baz shouted back up, ..."Who said you could use the tree house and me rope and make a swing?" .... Our Colin said, "We didn't think you'd mind." .... To which Baz shouted back up, ... "Mind? We'll see if I mind when you come down ... that's if I let you come down ya little ???????, I'll probably just batter you all how's that?" ... and then started laughing ... Well Baz did bully us and other kids a lot so we were pretty scared ...

Now Baz and his girlfriend were taking turns on the swing for ages ... And every so often Baz would shout up to us in the tree house, "Come on down I'm a waiting to have me some fun." ... Now Oggy started worrying about how late it was getting and was more worried about getting in trouble off his Mam and Dad than he was getting a belt or two off Baz ...

Then our Colin said, "I know! I've got me little hacksaw knife in me pocket." ... This is a knife that our Colin used to cut bits of inner tubes up to make patches to fix punctures on bike wheels ....

Where was I? ... Oh yeah ... So while Baz was swinging happily on the rope swing, Colin was happily cutting through the rope on the swing as the rope went over the thick branch just outside the entrance to the tree house ..... Then suddenly ...Yep you got it. Snap goes the rope, and Baz went wheeeee ... right into the mud of the swamp with an almighty splash ....

Which then gave us the chance to get down out of the tree house and peg it ... That's Manchester slang that means run like mad .... back home ... Which we did ...

Oggy got home in time as did Ayo, me and our Col, who told me Dad what had happened ... So when Baz and his girlfriend got to our house me Dad played hell with him ... Shouted at him in other words ...

The tree house was ok till the winter when it was spotted by the farmer through all the leaves falling off the old oak tree .... who just ripped it down ....

Hope and trust you could follow this memory and enjoyed the trip down misty old memory lane again ... Hope to catch you again on the next trip ... Thank you for keeping me company again ....

One day two of me pals were crossing a field full of cows when one pal said, "Look at that flock of cows over there." .... Me other pal said ... "Don't be stupid .... herd of cows!" ... So the first pal said ... "'Course I've heard of cows, there's a flock of them over there!"

9

<u>How I met Arthur</u>

This morning I got up and had a cuppa soup with toast for breakfast ... The sunlight was breaking through the thin summer curtains of our living room window ....

Sara, my wife, asked, "Well what shall we do on this lovely sunny day then?" ... "Um," I said, "You know I've told you some of my memories of playing in the fields and woods near the airport when I was a kid? ... Well what about me taking you to see some of those places?" ... Sara said, "Oh yeah, I would be honoured." ...

So we made some butties and a flask then put some cheesy biscuits along with them in the bag on the back of my mobility scooter and then Sara put a packet of baby wipes along with a bottle of cola in her bag on the back of her mobility scooter ... and then we got dressed and ready for our day out ...

After moving from Hulme in Manchester due to the slum clearance of the time we moved to Ravenscar Crescent in Woodhouse Park, a suburb of

Wythenshawe, next to what was then Ringway Airport ... Within days of arriving I had made a few friends on the Crescent ...

And we had established a focal meeting and playing area like we had done on the old local crofts in Hulme .... The one we used we simply called the Farmer's Field, which was an overgrown field situated behind the five rows of flats leading back from the Crescent to the field ... On the other side of the field was Ringway Road and a big pub called The Airport Hotel

Hope this information helps, as we travel back in time to the days and places of my childhood on my mobility scooter as my misty old memory train ....

We arrived at the Farmer's Field and I pointed out some old landmarks that still remain to be seen, like the remnants of the old pathways, and the bushes that now had grown into large trees ...

Then Sara poured us both a cuppa out of the flask ... As she did this, through the bubbling of the brew falling into the cup, I heard some distant echoing laughs and shouting from children playing in the still overgrown grass of the field ... It was then I realised these were the echoing voices of my childhood pals running around in the memories in my mind, which made me think of the story I am now going to tell you of how I met my life long friend Arthur ...

I'll just have some of me brew and get back to you ... Hey, you have one too please before we start ... Hi again me friend ... Who wants a ride down memory lane with me? ... You do? ... Well come on then ...

One sunny morning just before the whit week holidays came to an end ... Some of me old pals called for me to play out ... They were Linda .. Maureen .. Ronnie .. Billy .. Bobby .. Mike .. Dave .. Jack .. Tony E .. Eddy ... and me, Tosh ...

So just as kids do, we wandered off to our local play area, known locally as the Farmer's Field ... Which was situated at the back of the flats at the back of Ravenscar Crescent where I lived ... Between there and Ringway Road by the approach lights ... Not far from where the plane crashed on Shadowmoss Road back in 1957, just before the time of this story ...

Anyway, we all entered the field and headed over to the right where there was a dead tree and then sat down by the tree and made plans of what we were going to do that day ... Well the girls decided they were going to get some dinner for us lads, pretend dinner of course ... As they set off they were joined by another girl called Margaret ... So the girls headed off slapping their hips believing they were riding horses ...

Then us lads went further across the field to the bushes near Ringway Road to make us a den and we headed off slapping our hips too thinking we were riding a horse ... I think you know what I mean ha ha ha ... Anyway, we made us a hiding place and a den under those bushes just by bending and tying the thin branches together ... And clearing a space on the floor and made a small circle of stones ready to make us a little pretend fire ...

But the girls still hadn't come back yet, so we decided to send out a small patrol to look for them ... Which was Bill, Mike and Ronnie ... and the rest of us just carried on fixing up our new den ...

Then came a shout ... The patrol had returned with the girls all safe and rode into us camp, the boys slapping their hips, and immediately all fell to the ground at the den entrance, in a circle surrounding a ball of dead grass and leaves bunched tightly together that the girls had in their hands and arms ...

So the rest of us being soldiers as we were marched the few feet over to them to see what they had fetched back .... Well, the girls opened the bundle and inside it were all these tiny pink things that were wriggling and crawling all over the grass and leaf bundle the girls had made for them ... "What are they?" ... We all murmured and whispered ... But none of us knew for sure ... Anyway, we found out the next day that these tiny little pink things were baby field mice ....

Back to the story ... The girls insisted on taking the tiny things back home and most of the soldiers escorted them home ... While Ronnie, Mike, Eddy and me waited for them to come back ... But none of them came back ...

While we were waiting some lads we didn't know came riding by our camp slapping their hips ... So we came out of our den in the bushes and stopped them, saying, "Halt! Who goes there?" ... But they wouldn't say who they were ... So we tried to tell them to clear off, saying, "It's our land, clear off!" ...

But sure enough a fight started ... Then two of the strangers ran off, with our lads chasing after them and left me and this other kid to sort things out... So we called a truce and I arranged to meet up with him the next day in the Farmer's Field by the dead tree at about 12 o'clock ...

Which I did, and this lad's name was Arthur, Ampy, and we became mates ... Then he joined our gang ... and to this day, over sixty years later, we are still the best of mates ... And still, when we go out anywhere, for a giggle, slap our hips for old times sake ...

But now, as we headed home, Sara and me, I felt a tear roll down my cheek as I realised those echoing voices from my childhood and those special events of this day over sixty years earlier, were now just an old man's memory ...

Those legs of ours we believed to be our horses are a bit limp these days, and all the hip slapping in the world won't make our legs go any faster ha ha ha ...

10

<u>The stinging wasps of Shadow Wood</u>

Well after meeting up with Arthur the next day at the old dead tree at twelve noon as agreed, and as some of our gang were coming in to the field, Arthur nervously invited me and the few mates of mine to come and see his special place where he and his mates played ...

This place, he explained, was a large wood called Shadow Wood, which was very close to where Arthur lived ... And he explained there were always some of his mates in the woods and said maybe we could join gangs and play games together in the woods ..... Well we agreed and off we trotted for about a mile to Shadow Wood ...

When we arrived, sure enough there were some of Arthur's gang playing in the woods ... Arthur called them over, had a chat and we all agreed we would join us two gangs together to make one large gang and straight away we made plans to start playing a game together in Shadow Wood .....

Come on now and hop aboard our memory train folks and let's see where it takes us ... It's very misty out there so we can't see very much and we are going a bit too fast ... Arh, that's better, we're slowing down and the mist is clearing away ...

Now we've stopped and everyone is getting off the train ... We look around and we're in the middle of a very large wood with a small pond to our right ... Then us gang starts to gather round and we can see who's here with us ...

There was Billy, Bobby, Ronnie, Mic, Dave, Stan, Jimmy, Malc, Bryan D, Eddy D, Ayo, Johnny B, Paul C, Arthur, Steve, Tony E, Ginge, and me and me dog Smokey ... And a few girls ... Linda, Ruth and me sister Pam ...

So we had us a good crew this day, and we were in Shadow Wood by the flats on Shadowmoss Road ... Well, we decided to split into two groups and we were going to play at war ... The English versus the Japs ...

So we picked Linda, Ruth and me sister Pam to be the medics ... and made a little corral type square made up of ferns about two feet high and about six feet square ... For them to put the injured and captured soldiers from both sides in to pretend to take care of them .....

Then one group, the English Army, set off into the woods first led by Stan ... And built and made dens and traps to try and capture us, the Japs, led by Ronnie ... So we set off next and made our hide outs and traps ... When we were done we shouted across the woods to each other ... The usual, coming ready or not ... To set the war game off ...

They, the English, crawled round on their bellies through the bushes and ferns trying to sneak up on us ... But we did the same ...

You could hear when some of the lads saw each other cos you'd hear pee yown, pee yown, pee yown ... Shooting noises we made with us mouths and pointing our pretend gun that was just made with a small branch really ...Which we used to try and shoot, capture and overpower the enemy with ...

Well, after about an hour or so we were getting nowhere but we were getting hungry, thirsty and tired ... So we decided to call all in all in ... And met up with the girls at their base ...

Where we got a little fire going, chilled out and started showing off to the girls by imitating film stars ... Running and trying rolling over tactics like they had seen in the movies ...

But suddenly the girls and a couple of the boys started screaming and waving their arms around in the air like mad ... Then everyone was doing the same and started to run ... Even me dog was running and started to yelping ...

Well what had happened was someone, while running, jumping and rolling over on the floor had busted open a wasp's nest ... and they were so mad at us, buzzing and stinging all of us and me poor dog Smokey ...

We all got home by the skin of us teeth ... But full of stings which by now, were like big blisters ... Well me Mam put toothpaste and vinegar on our stings ... mine and our Pam's that is ... I don't know how the rest of the gang's Mams sorted them out ... I just know we had been stung several times by these wasps ...

Even today if I go out near any woods I look to see if

there's any wasps flying around ... If there are I keep a wide berth away from that place ...

Hope you liked this painful memory I have shared with you ... Thank you for keeping me company on me journey back to me childhood days ... It's time for me to buzz off now ... bbbbuuuuzzzzzzzz .....

Stay safe and stay away from those nasty little yellow and black flying things called wasps ... Ouch! .... Ouch! ....

It hurts just thinking about them .... And I reckon most people have been attacked and stung by these little devils at some point in their lives eh? .... Don't you?

11

<u>Tarzan and Jane in Shadow Wood</u>

After the stinging problems last time we were in these woods, me, Arthur and the gang decided to go back to Shadow Wood and make a new den in a different part of the wood, well away from those wasps ...

So who fancies going on another trip down memory lane? ... You do? ... Well hop on board and let's go eh?

The weekend just before the summer holiday started me and me mates had gone over to Shadow Wood near Arthur's house to have another go at making a den and a base in the wood and play games ...

Anyway after we got to the woods ... Karen, one of the older girls in our gang, told us all to sit down which we did ... Then she told us a story while some of us sat on an old rotten log, about her going to the pictures with her Dad the night before and watching a Tarzan film ... and then she told us the story line as best she could remember it ... and how Tarzan and his wife Jane lived with the animals in the jungle ....

Well I think you know what's coming next ... Yep ...
We made us a clearing and a new den ... Then took us
tops off, put them inside the den on the floor ... and
now we were jungle men and monkeys ... And Ginger
was Tarzan and Karen was Jane ... Now the scene was
set for them to live in their den ...

While the rest of us split up into two groups .... One
group was tribes men who wanted to capture Jane and
take her prisoner, to lure out Tarzan to capture him too
.... So we all went off into two groups pretending we
could hear and see all types of the wild animals .....
Half of us were monkeys, Tarzan's friends, climbing
trees and running through the ferns making monkey
noises ... And the other half were the bad guy tribes
men ... who were just breaking branches and making a
mess of the woods ....

The game was that the bad guys had to try and steal
away Jane by distracting Tarzan any way they could
away from Jane so the tribes men could snatch her
away ...

As Tarzan had the strength of ten men that meant no
tribes man could stand up to Tarzan alone ..... So the
jungle men would throw sticks and bits of soil at the

den, then run off and then run back passed the doorway of Tarzan's den to try and draw him out ... Risking life and limb to draw Tarzan away from Jane ... After a while Tarzan had got really mad and chased off some tribes men waving a conifer branch at them as he chased them away ....

But some tribes men were in hiding in some nearby bushes so as Tarzan chased their mates off passed the ones in hiding ... the ones that had been in hiding ran out and into Tarzan and Jane's den and grabbed Jane ... Who now had started screaming for her Tarzan to come back and rescue her ... Help! Help! Help! ...

But all seemed lost now ..... Jane had been taken and Tarzan on his own out in the open jungle was no match for all those tribes men .... But wait ...

Tarzan clenched his fists and began beating on his chest like a gorilla, gave out a couple of yells and calls and then all the monkeys came running through the ferns and swinging on the branches in the trees to Tarzan's aid ... Then along with Tarzan, planned and carried out their own daring attack on the jungle men's hideout and released Jane by untying her and leading her off to safety back to Tarzan's home, the den ...

All the tribes men ran off into the forest .... Whilst all the monkeys gathered round Tarzan and Jane and celebrated their victory over the tribes men ... All along one of the gang named Billy shouted out a running commentary of what was happening and how the story would unfold .... Bet you remember how a gang member used to do the commentary on certain games you played eh? ...

Then the story was over ... We all gathered back together, had us a chat about what game we would play the following day, or whenever we could all meet up again ....

Then we all went home tired, dirty and hungry ... I had a wash down, then had me tea and told me Mam about the game in the woods we had played that day ... Then off to bed, said me prayers and fell asleep

Did you ever play similar type games with your pals in your local woods, crofts or play areas? ...

Here's a few things I remember from back in me childhood years ... A lot of me mates would have them in their pockets, so if we all emptied us pockets on the ground here's what you'd find most of the time ....

Hope these things bring back memories for you too .... And I'll bet you can think of lots of other things as well .... Ok here we go ... A home made catapult ... a magnifying glass ... a compass ... a ball of string ... a tea spoon ... a pen knife ... a sheath knife ... a peice of carbolic soap in a cloth ... a Box of matches ... loose pebbles ... a peice of ribbon ... a comb ... a bit of old chewing gum ... a hanky ... a few hair grips ... some marbles ... a couple of old conkers ... And the good old cork from a bottle that we would burn to do our faces up and blacken under us eyes to play comandos ...

Then we had bottles of corporation pop ... Drippin or jam butties ... And if we were lucky one of us kids would have a few sweets to share out ... (Yeah man!)

Eee bar gum ... Great long ago childhood memories .... And our great imaginations which led to the great memorable games we played.

12

<u>Two kids in a grave</u>

Here is a bit of a different type of memory I wish to share with you ... It's a little bit spooky ....

One of me mate Arthur's elder brothers had recently got married and had rented a bed sit for himself and his new bride ... On Wilbraham Road, Chorlton Cum Hardy ....

And Arthur asked me if I fancied having a long walk over to see his brother with him ... So I said, "Yeah, go on then" ... Because Arthur said, "Don't worry, he'll give us the money to get a bus home, no problem." ...

Anyway, it was quite a walk but we got there after about two hours and called to see Arthur's brother but sadly for us there was no one home ... The land lord said Arthur's brother had been out all day and the land lord had no idea where he was ... Or what time he would be back ...

What a blow this was to me and me mate Arthur as it's a good five mile walk from our houses to Wilbraham

Road, and we were both tired and were hoping to cadge the bus fare back home off Arthur's brother ...

Arh well, it was getting late but it was a very warm summer evening so we set off back home ...

But decided to be mischievous and cut through the allotments at Hough End to annoy the old gardeners for a laugh ....

But as soon as we had got off Princess Parkway, the main road home and entered the allotments, two policemen that had been chatting to one of the old gardeners shouted at us, saying, "Come here you two little shits! What you doing in here?" ...

So we ran off through the allotments, through the cabbages, lettuce and whatever else they had been growing towards Southern Cemetery ...

Then cut through the grave yard with the policemen in hot pursuit ... And we kept looking back over our shoulders to see if these two coppers were catching up to us .... But no they weren't ...

But then suddenly as we ran across an old tarpaulin the ground disappeared and we both fell into an opened grave ... Which was about eight foot or so deep ... And we stood on the tarpaulin that had covered the grave and was now under our feet ,..

We very soon realised we were in a grave ... Aaarrrrhhhh! .... And we really panicked and tried us best to get out but it seemed like forever we were down there ...

Then there was a loud crack beneath us and we fell yet deeper in the grave, ... As what was underneath us must have been an old coffin that broke which made us really panic and suddenly we were both out of that grave and leaning with our backs on a head stone on the next grave ...

We were knackered and full of mud but at last somehow we had gotten out .... And it was now going dusk and had gone pretty cloudy and dark when we heard? ..... WHOOOOOOO .... WHOOOOOOO .... WHAAAAAA ... WHAAAA ...

It was those two policemen trying to scare us into running and revealing where we had been hiding .... By this time the light was fading very fast and I was terrified ....

Then Arthur, me mate, started to make similar noises back to those policemen ... Well believe it or not, these two coppers ran off faster than a speeding bullet ... ha ha ha ... Just goes to show though, even the police have strange experiences and get scared like the rest of us ...

Me and me mate Arthur still talk about this event after all these years and we wonder what these policemen told their bosses and their work mates when they got back to the station? ... The story didn't end there though ....

As we went on our way when the police had run off ... We noticed as we got out of the cemetery on the other side near Barlow Moor Road a strange bluey grey mist following us down Barlow Moor Road ... Until we got near to the crematorium entrance where it just faded and disappeared ...

When we told Arthur's brother a few days later about what had happened and about the bluey grey misty light, he said it was the Blue Lady that haunts the cemetery ... And locally it was a very well known ghost ....

Well I don't know about that ... But what I do know is it scared the living daylights out of us at the time and I don't want to see it again ... We don't know what it was ... But it sure was a very strange thing

We were just about ten years old at the time ... Young, gullible and easily scared ... I have never heard of anyone else mentioning this light so I kept me gob shut all these years till now .....

Sleep tight tonight and stay away from cemetaries after dark 'cause who knows what might happen or what you may see or hear.

13

<u>Me, our Colin and us pigeons</u>

Well howdy partner ... Glad you're back and hope you're sitting comfortably and do you fancy another trip down memory lane? ... C'mon then .....

Well this memory starts around August time 1959 ... First of all I'd better fill you in with the background to the story ....

We, me and our Colin, me Dad's youngest brother, are only three years different in age and whenever we could we would ride to each other's houses and play and stay the night ... Me at me Ninny Ratcliff's flat and our Colin at me Dad's house with us ....

Riding was flippin' tough and took a long time ... We couldn't get the bus as we, our families and us kids, never had the money ...

We had a go a few times at making up bikes from scrap bikes out of the canal, the River Irwell, or wherever we could find old, dumped and broken bikes, which we were pretty good at getting and fixing up ....

But they were never the best and never lasted too long
... But hey, they did the job for us many a time ....
Until the bearing went in the wheels, then it was time
to get rid and just make another bike up using the
same frame ... I think you know what I mean ....

If you know Manchester you'll know the route we
would take .... All the way down Princess Parkway,
onto Greenwood Road, onto the long black path, then
onto Cornishway, then cut through the housing estate
and wham, done! ... And visa versa to go the other
way .... It took ages and as kids was pretty hard
work ......

I lived in Woodhouse Park near Ringway Airport and
Colin lived with his Mam, Me Gran, on Jackson
Street, Hulme ... About nine miles apart .... That's a
long way for kids to ride, and yeah, on us own ... No
numpty men about in those days, not that bothered us
anyway ....

Well this August Saturday I rode to our Colin's ... You
know, at me Ninny Ratcliff's .... And he was playing
on the veranda with some string, a small box and an

old rusty budgie cage out of the Irwell ....

I asked him what he was doing and he said, "Making traps." .... "Uh .... What for?" I said ....."You'll see when we get up in the morning." Colin replied ... As I said, whenever I went to me Ninny Ratcliff's I stayed the night ...

Anyway Colin showed me how to tie hoops in string and bend over small pieces of cane he had cut down into strips .... I reckon about twelve inches long .... So we made a few of them till Ninny shouted us indoors for tea ... Can't remember what we had ...

Oh, forgot to tell you, me Ninny and Colin lived on the ground floor of the flats ... Thank goodness! ... Imagine climbing up those concrete steps after such a long ride Phew! ... No chancy Nancy! .....

Anyway, we had us tea and listened to the radio ... No TV back then, we were all too poor ....

Well I must have fell asleep for the night as the next memory I have is setting up these pieces of cane and string with our Colin ... About four of them, about three feet apart, and on the last one Colin had leaned one box over onto another box with a little piece of cane between them ....

Then Colin went back indoors and came out with some tiny bits of bread ..... and sprinkled them round the traps .... He got back on the veranda and was holding a piece of string ...

Well it seemed within moments pigeons came to eat the bread ... The traps were set off one by one, even the one Colin had the piece of string in his hand for .... And we had captured three pigeons ...

Then Colin jumped over the veranda, grabbed them and stuffed them into this budgie cage ..... Then took them indoors and came back out with the budgie cage empty .... Then did the whole thing again ...... and again ... till we had about eight pigeons that were good enough for Colin's standards ....

When we finished Colin took me indoors off the veranda and into his bedroom, where there was a big black wooden box which our Barry, the next one up in age from Colin, had made ..... Corr! .... This is hard work explaining but we're nearly there! .....

Right, Colin had a friend who raced pigeons and had told our Colin how you get them to home ... That means when you let them go from wherever you have taken them they will always find their way home ...

Hope you're following me .... Corr! I need a brew and a paracetamol! ... Back in a minute! ...... Back now! ...

Ok then, according to our Colin, after you have captured young pigeons you put them in a dark box with a small slit in the bottom at the front of the box about one inch high for the light, air, water and food they need ...

Keep them locked in for about a week ... Then open the slit about another inch and keep them fed and watered for about another three days ... Then let them out .... So that's what we both did ...

Anyway, after that we would send each other messages with the pigeons .... Seemed to work great all summer long .... Both me and our Colin had built small pigeon lofts for our pigeons but one morning I got up and all my birds were dead .....

Me Dad said at the time that they probably died of

fright, maybe a fox had been staring in at them through the loft vent .... But the next time I saw our Colin his four birds had died too around the same time .... So we never knew why they had died and never tried to keep homing pigeons again ....

Slowly Colin and I drifted apart as he carried on playing with his pals up in Hulme and I just played out with my pals I had made down here in Wythenshawe ....

Looking back we were growing up fast and our childhood years, unbeknown to us both were drawing swiftly to an end ......

And looking back thinking of those pigeons, maybe these birds had some kind of illness or disease, I don't know ... But it was a shock and upsetting to see them dead ....

Did you, your family or pals try things out like this back in the day when you were kids? .... Hope you liked this memory that I've shared and didn't get too bored reading it .... I ain't too good at explaining things as you have probably noticed by now... But I'm trying me best ...

Though I never really had a go at pigeons again twenty years later I was well into breeding budgies as was me late youger brother Steve ... Our Steve bred pieds and even had a go at breeding cockatiels ... Not me though, I preferred the smaller birds so I just bred lutinos, albinos and blues ...

We both did pretty well for a good few years until the time we packed in breeding birds due to the fact that so many people had now started to lose interest in having budgies as a pets in their homes ... And the craze for keeping and breeding tropical fish took hold ... Bet you had a tropical fish tank in your house back in the day.

Arh well, We all do us best to entertain ourselves and our families .... These days everyone seems to spend their lives looking at their mobile phones ... Well I guess that's life I suppose ... I wonder what pets or hobbies you kept or had as a kid back in the day? ... Or what you may have had in later years?

14

How to make a

good old fashioned flicking bogey

Here are the instructions on how to make good old fashioned flicking bogeys ... OK Let's start to make us bogey together eh? ...

If you have some space in a garage or a shed to work in that'll be great, just in case it rains ... Now let's get a brush and make a good clean space by sweeping up ... Can't make one with a lot of clutter and dirt about can we? ...

Next get two sets of large pram wheels on axles with good tyres on them ... Now get some wire wool and give the wheel shafts and wheel spokes a real good rubbing down untill they're silver looking ...

Now hopefully you have some spray paint ... Lay some paper down on the floor and paint the wheels, spokes and axles ... Ok so far ... Then while the paint dries ...

Go and get a good sized plank of wood about six inch

by two inch and cut it down to about five foot six inches long ... And give it a real good sanding down till it looks like brand new smooth timber with no splinters ...

Next you'll need to cut another piece of the same timber about two foot six inches long as the cross beam for the back wheels and then sand this timber down to the same high finish ...

Then screw this timber to the main timber so now you'll have a large tee shaped frame ... Now using u-bolts attach the back wheels to the cross timber ...

Then cut another timber roughly the same size as the first cross beam ... and sand this down too ... Now we're getting close eh? ...

Find the centre of this timber by drawing a line from corner to corner that makes a x shape then drill a hole in the centre ... Then approximately one foot from the front of the main long base board drill a hole in that too ...

And using a six inch bolt with washers between the boards attach this cross member ... And now, as with the rear wheels, attach the front wheels with u-bolts ...

Now be sure to check all fixings are safe and tight ... Then oil the wheels and the bolt hole for the front wheels ... Looking good now or what? ...

Just need to add a steering line then clean up all our sawdust and mess then away we go! ... Yeah man! ...

And now for special effects ... Get your Dad or Mam to make you a wooden seat with a back rest, then fix it to the back cross beam ...

And heat up a poker on a fire and burn marks into the wood to look like black flames ... Wow yippee! Look at this baby now eh? ...

BEST BLOW YOUR NOSE NOW TO CLEAR THE MUCK AND DUST OUT ... WOW! JUST LOOK AT THE SIZE OF THEM FLICKING BOGEYS? ... ha ha ha ...

HOPE YOU ENJOYED THE BUILD PROJECT.

15

<u>Shopping on tick, the poorly rabbit</u>

Whoosh! ... What was that? Was it a train? A rocket? Or a speeding bullet? ..... Nope, it was just you running away from me on me misty wobbly old memory horse with yet another old memory to share .....

Just let me dismount and slap me hip so I can trot over to me rocking chair ... Well it's me chair really that rocks and wobbles a bit cos it's got a castor wheel missing .... And I'm too tight to pay for it to be fixed ....

Well get your butties, brew and a chocolate biscuit ready to dunk ... and get your feet up as we drift back in time down the forever fading memory lane ....

This memory starts on a misty summer's morning when two of me mates called for me to play out ... Ayo, pronounced Eye-yo ..... and another mate called Tony ....

So I called back into the house to me Mam, who was

down the hallway in the kitchen, ... "Eh Mam, is it ok if I can play out?" ...... Me Mam shouted back, "No, not yet, you need to go to the shops and see if you can get some stuff on tick for me first." .... "Ok Mam." I said .... So me Mam wrote a note ... and gave me a cloth bag to put the shopping in ......

So off to the shops me and me mates galloped, slapping us hips as normal as we went ......

So at the first shop I went in and gave them the note and the bag and the man whose shop it was got a tin of beans, a tin of peas, some eggs and wrapped up some bacon and put the shopping in me bag for me ...

Then he wrapped up in a brown paper bag what I now know was cigs ... and he said, "Be careful with this, gently put it in your pocket." ... Then gave me the note off me Mam back and put a note of his own in me bag ... Then said, "Tell your Mam to call in on Saturday." ....

All went well there ... So we nipped around the corner to the green grocers ... and gave him the other note off me Mam and he just gave it me back saying, "Tell your Mam she ain't paid for the last lot yet." .... And asked me to ask her to pop in for a chat ...

So off home I went with me mates ... I gave me Mam
the shopping I had got for her ... I told her what the
green grocer had said ... Me Mam went beserk and
started cursing and swearing ... Then blamed me
saying, "You have been cheeky to him haven't
you?" ... I said, "No Mam I wasn't." .... Arh well, she
then told me to get out and play then with your
mates ...

Which I did ... and we went to a wood at the back of
Manchester Airport where there was a gun turret at the
side of the path that led to the old entrance to Styal
Woods and down the steps to the wire swing bridge
over the River Bollin ...... This wood was known
locally to us kids as Turret Woods ... Just for reference
for those of you who knew the area back then ....

Anyway, we played inside the old gun turret and in
the wood, just doing what kids do, climbing trees,
looking for sticks to pretend were rifles or swords and
vee branches that were good enough to make catapults
with ...

Then we, me and Tony, ended up making a fire inside

the gun turret while Ayo collected some fire wood ...

Then we heard him shout, "Help! Help! Come on you two help! HELP!" .... So we ran outside but couldn't see him and shouted back, "Where are you?" ... Ayo shouted back, "Where are you?" ... As he came trudging through the bushes to the right with something grey and bouncing about inside his jacket ... "Help me," he said, "It'll get away and it's hurt." ....

At this point one of us took us jacket off ... Can't remember if it was me or Tony, and helped Ayo to get this grey thing from inside his jacket and wrapped it up in one of our jackets .... After investigating it .... it turned out to be a rabbit ...

But where its eyes should be there were just blooded holes .... So not knowing what was wrong with it, we decided to take it home ....

When we got home we put it in the washing boiling bin .... That's a bin that our Mams would light underneath and boil our white clothes in ... Obviously it was empty and had no water in it either ....

Tony went and got his Dad to come and see it and Ayo went home as he didn't want to get into trouble for being late home ...

Tony's Dad wasn't sure what was wrong with it and while we, me, Tony and his Dad were looking at the rabbit and chatting, me Dad came home from work and saw us round the back of the house and had a look at the rabbit himself ... But he too didn't know what was wrong ....

I'm not sure where he came from or if someone had sent for him ... But a local bobby on a bike came down the path and had a look at the poor rabbit, then had a chat with our Dads and said it's a rabbit with myxomatosis ... Just wrap it up in an old pillowcase or something and I'll take it back to the station with me ....

Well back then the police station was on the corner of Braintree Road and Cornishway ... Not far from our house ...

Well off he went with the rabbit and we cried asking, "What's going to happen to it?" ... Tony's Dad said, "Don't worry, they'll fix it and put it back in the woods and its Mam and Dad will come and take it home and they'll live happily ever after ......

Every time we went back to the Turret Wood we would all look for that rabbit, or other rabbits, but never found any ......

I know why now .... It's that evil myxomatosis... And sadly both these old pals, Tony and Ayo, have now passed away too .... But they live on in this old memory of mine ....

Thank you for reading my little memory ... Hope you liked it ... Bet you have some fond old memories with some of your old pals like mine too eh?

16

New territory and the scary screams

Clipperty clop clipperty clop .... gee up ... come on now girl ... Not much further to go now and we'll be out of Injun country .... Slappin' me hip as usual I said, ... "Cum on I know you're tired lass but I'm sure we can make it." ....

Well it was one of the last weekends of this summer and it was a very hot and humid sunny day for this time of year ... And we, me horse and me, had set off for our new den that me and me mates had started to build earlier on the weekend before ....

Nearby the power station and footbridge over the railway lines at the side of Reynald Chains factory on Styal Road ...... We, all the gang, had arranged to meet up on this, the following weekend and to bring some supplies ... food, drinks and any old bed sheets or blankets are Mams may be throwing out ....

Well I had me school satchel on me back with two old mineral bottles full of corporation pop ... For the younger folk reading my story ... It's what we used to

call tap water back in the day ... I also had some dry
toast as we had no margarine in at home or dripping to
put on it .... So the toast was stuffed in me satchel
too ... But bar heck it was heavy ....

Our new den was in a field next to the railway lines
and footbridge heading south from Heald Green
railway station for those who knew the area back
then .... And we had made us den by the old cars at the
side of the pigswill pond near what we believed to be
a large farm building ....

As I approached I gave out the gang call wit ... wit ...
Which is the sound of a Pee Wit ... or maybe better
known as a Lapwing bird ... That nests on the
ground ... Well Mike and Eddy came riding up
slapping their hips and escorted me into our camp ....
and I got them to lift me heavy bag off me back ...

While they were doing this I noticed how lovely the
camp looked compared to last weekend ... There were
two old cars side by side but about three feet apart and
the gang had got a large old piece of canvas out of a
local wrecked barn and fixed it across the two cars
with a couple of old planks, one at the front and one at
the back so it was a really firm and good looking roof

between the cars ....

And what made it look real nice and special was the girls ... Linda, Maureen, Maggie and Pauline had made really long daisy chains with daisies and buttercups alternate and had threaded them all around the outskirts of the roof and the entrance to the den ...

The other kids were inside the old abandoned cars tidying the insides up and making them comfy .... Jimmy, the eldest one of the gang at the time had got a small fire going with his spy glass .... So we were all settling down now to have a bit of a drink, grub and a chat ...

When we heard some loud bangs and what sounded like a woman screaming ... So being really brave and having a full troop of soldiers .... We all dived for cover ha ha ha ... Told you we were a brave lot .... And we all hid the best we could ... Told you we were a tough lot dint I? ... ha ha ha ...

Anyway, after a few minutes and a lot of whispering .... Jimmy and Eddy, being the eldest lads and the general and captain asked for volunteers to ride out to find out what it was ..... So being a brave

old cavalry group we all stood up to volunteer ...
NOT! ....

So the girls being weak and feeble as girls were back
then asked, "Shall we go and have a look?" Well the
two brothers Bobby and Billy that was with us that
day said ... "If a couple more come with us we'll go,
we can't let the girls go." .... So little Ronnie said "I'll
come along." And dumb old me said, "Me too sir." ...

So we lined up ready to trot off to investigate when
there was a loud bang followed by the screams
again ... Well this time we really hit the dirt ..... Then
after a few seconds and a lot of whispering again ....

Jimmy said, "Come on now soldiers stiff upper lip
you know we're British soldiers." ... "Hang about,
aren't we cowboys?" Billy said ... "Shut up." said
Eddy ... You're the patrol, go and check out what the
danger is." ......

So again being really really brave we got down on our
hands and knees and started to crawl across the field
to where the noises seemed to be coming from ... Well
we had gone about fifty yards and were by a ditch and
some bushes when again we heard a loud bang

followed by some loud screams again ....

Please, if you're at all squeamish, at this point go and play Candy Crush on Facebook or some other game .... You have been warned .... Right then, on we go with the story ....

Anyway, where was I? ...... Oh yeah ... With hearing the bang and sreams again we lay as flat as we possibly could to the ground ....

Then again after the noise and screams subsided off we crawled again passed the bushes and saw a large concrete building with a steel corrugated roof on just about another fifty yards on over the field .... The bangs and screams happened again but this time we realised it was coming from inside this building ... Then silence ......

So again onward we crawled and got to the building just in time for the bangs and screaming to start again ...... So Ronnie, being the smallest, asked us to peg him up to a tiny window in the side of the building to take a look for what the noises were ... Then Bobby said, "Hang on lads there's a door down there ... and there was, a small wooden door just about ten feet further down the side of the building .... We carefully edged up to the door as tight as we could to the wall and opened the door a couple of inches and four heads, one above the other, were then looking in the opening of the door ...

We saw a man dragging a big heavy chain across the floor followed by another man with what looked like an electric drill ... They walked either side of a steel fence, then just stood there,not saying a word ... Then we saw a third man leading a giant pig on some kind of a lead ....

Then the man with the chain wrapped it around the pig's back legs, slammed a gate behind him and pulled the chain using the gate as a lever, which made the pig squeal ...

Then the man with the drill looking thing put it to the pig's head and pulled the trigger .... I'll not go on with any more details ... Just to say within minutes that poor pig was shaking all over and being cut up for the butcher's shop ....

Well feeling very sick, upset and scared we all ran back to our den as fast as we could ... Then told the others what we had seen and we all just ran off home with no hip slapping this time ... Now scared and crying our eyes out ....

We left all our stuff behind there ... I even left me school satchel behind and never went back for it ...... Nor ever played in those fields again ....

When I first married me Sara I shared with her this memory as I have with all me other memories and diary entries that I have now started to share with you lovely folk reading me book ....

Hope me sharing this memory hasn't bothered you too much .... This is just another one of those unforgettable memories that has been branded on my mind forever ....

17

Truck crash and first trip to Alderley Edge

Hi again folks ... There's nothing too exciting really about this memory ... But it's a memory I wish to share with you ... I trust you're in fine fettle and sitting comfortably ... Ready to hop on board for another trip down the misty old memory lane ...

I was reminded recently about Heald Green railway station and the many fields around there ... They were a large expanse of fields that us kids from Woodhouse Park would travel to and play in them ...

For as the estates of Wythenshawe and Manchester Airport grew ever larger the play areas for us kids locally grew ever smaller ...

The reminder I was given was about the old path that used to run down the side of the railway lines all the way down to Wilmslow and Alderley Edge where there are some pot holes ...

Anyway, what I recall is a very strange day when me

and some of the gang were playing in the field next to the railway station that lies between the station and Heald Green hardware shop on the opposite side of the field ... Well here is how this memory unfolds ...

Jimmy and his older brother Brian, some of the older members of our gang, had been sent by their Mam to Heald Green hardware shop for some paraffin as the local one near home, Higginson's on Cornishway, had run out of paraffin ..... Anyway, me and some of me pals, John, Billy, Bobby, Ronnie and Linda were playing in the field ....

When we heard one almighty bang ... "Wow! What was that?" We asked each other ... Then went to investigate where we thought the bang had come from ... It seemed to be from the hardware shop ... Then as we all climbed over the wooden gate from the field onto the road .....

We saw all these adults running towards the shop .... Which now had some smoke rising from its front entrance ... Then we saw and heard men shouting, "Make way! Make way! Make a space!" ...

Then as we neared the shop front we saw some men

carrying an old man with blood running down his face and other men carrying a younger man away from the shop front towards the road that passed by the front of the shop ....

This is when we saw Jimmy and his older brother Brian in the crowd ... They saw us too and came over and told us what had happened ....

They told us that they had just been given a gallon of paraffin and were just about to pay for it when this pick up truck smashed into the shop ....

And they started laughing saying, "Look we got us paraffin for nowt and Brian had nicked a rope and torch off the back of the pick up truck." ... And now they were eager to get away from the shop

Now one of the brothers, I think it was Brian, went home with the paraffin and Jimmy said, "We got a rope and a torch, c'mon let's go pot holing." ... "What's pot holing?" I asked ... Jimmy said, "You'll see, it's fun! ... All we have to do is get there and the best way is to follow the railway lines south, c'mon!" ...

So we all climbed back over the wooden gate to the

field and we were on us way to another adventure .... So off we went, not having a clue where, or how far, this pot holing game was ...

Here's where I'll cut the story short ... We walked to this place called Alderley Edge following the railway lines which took us a couple of hours at least ...

So when we got there we were really tired and hot so we shaded under some trees and had a rest ... Then one of the gang went to a cottage near the entrance gate and asked if they could spare us some water please ....

Well these were lovely kind folk and they gave us all a nice cold cup of water each .... Then gave us two mineral bottles full of water too and said, "You'll probably need these later on." .... We said, "Thank you." ... And asked where we should go to find these pot holes as Jimmy didn't know ... He had just been told about the place ... Arrrrh! ...

The lady in the cottage said, "Follow the path and you'll see a large crack in the ground and that's the beginning of the mines." ....

Well, we did as instructed and sure enough arrived at a huge crack in the ground .... We now know this is known as Engine Vein mine shaft ....

Then we walked into this crack in the ground and as it went deeper so did we .... Until we came to a big drop in front of us ... Then in the dim torch light we spotted a spike head in the floor and decided to tie the rope which Jimmy and Brian nicked off the truck to it and see if we could climb down the rope further into the cave ...

Which we did in turn and when we had all climbed down to the bottom we shone the torch around ...

Wow! We all realised we now were in a giant cave so after a short time exploring the batteries in the torch started failing so we all climbed back out full of awe and amazement and headed off back home the way we had come following the railway lines home .....

When we got home we all got in deep trouble as we really hadn't noticed how dirty and muddy we had all gotten in those pot holes ...

But we all had fun and had made plans to go again

sometime in the future but with more ropes, torches, grub and water to explore more of those caves at Alderley Edge ....

I really hope you enjoyed this little pot holing memory with me .... I wonder if you have ever been pot holing or in a giant cave too? ....

Think it's time for me to have a brew and dunk a few biscuits now ... So my friend, till the next time we take a trip down memory lane, take good care of yourself.

18

<u>Len and his bird's eggs</u>

Here is another old memory I would like to share with you .....

Well I was told by one of the older gang leaders about a new kid that had moved into our turf from out of town ... And asked if I would call round to his house to check him out as all gangs did back then to make sure that they wouldn't end up being a problem for us .....

Like if they befriended some of us gang members and turned out to be a grass, you know, a tell tale on some of the naughty things we sometimes got up to ...

Anyway I called round to his house on Staithes Road, knocked on his door and asked him if he fancied playing out ... Then I welcomed him into the area, told him my name and he said his name was Len ....

Then we sat on his front door step and chatted ... That's when he told me his family had moved here to Wythenshawe from Cheetham Hill, near Heaton

Park .... And just like most of us had moved to Wythenshawe due to the demolition of the old streets and houses where he had lived ...

Then told me his family were Jewish and had come to England from Poland and they didn't have many friends and that they really didn't trust none Jews ...

Well I explained to him as best as I could about our gang ....With the many different nationalities we had in it .... And that everyone believes in God so we just get on with playing out together .... Ayo's family was from Africa, Otto's family was from Czechoslovakia, Hami from India, Syd from Jamaica ... Peter from France, and a good few of us from Ireland, Scotland, and Wales ... plus lots of Mancs eh ... Ha ha ha ... We started to laugh ....

Just as we started laughing Len's Dad came to the door, And asked Len, "Who is this then Son?" ... So Len told his Dad I was called Tony ... His Dad said, "I know," and chuckled .... Then said, "I have been listening to you two chatting for a while now." ... And Tony seems to be a nice lad ....

Len and his Dad spoke very good English though you

could tell they weren't Mancs ... His Dad said, "You'd best come in for your dinner now, so say goodbye to your friend." ... Len asked me if I would call back again tomorrow ... I said, "Yeah." And off I went home ....

I met big Tic Kelly, the big main leader of the gang and told him about Len ... He just said, "Fine, ... let me know how you get on tomorrow." ...

The next day I called around to Len's house but this time was invited indoors and up to his room where he told me he was an only child and he had no Mam so there was just him and his Dad living there ...

Then he told me what his hobby was, and that was collecting bird's eggs ..... Then shouted to his Dad, saying, "Is it ok if I show Tony my bird's egg collection?" ... His Dad simply shouted, "Go ahead it'll be fine." ...

Anyway Len then showed me a large dressing table looking thing with lots of drawers in it ... But the drawers were only about two inches deep ... The bottoms were lined with cotton wool but there were row after row of all colours and sizes of birds eggs in each drawer ... I have never seen anything like this before or since so I was stunned ....

But I asked Len where he had got all these eggs from and he simply said, "Out of bird's nests, just one out of each nest ... I've done it for years." ...

I am trying to keep this memory as short as I can and hope you don't find it boring ...

Len asked me if I knew anywhere local where there were hedge rows and/or clumps of trees .... So he could show me how to spot nests, collect and blow the eggs and start a collection along with his ....

Well of course I knew lots of these kind of places but would have to get permission off me Mam to travel to the woods and fields at the back of the Airport to show him ... Then told him I would call back again in the morning to take him if me Mam said it would be ok ...

So after going home, then calling to see and let some of the gang know what other things I had learned that night, I decided to take him to Styal Woods the next day ... But would take another mate with me to be sure I was safe and he wasn't a wrong un ....

Anyway, the next day me and me mate Mike called for Len and his Dad said it's ok for him to play out ... We headed off to Styal ... Well Len was looking in every hedgerow and tree on the way to Styal and collected a good few eggs ... But never took more than one egg out of each nest he found ...

Mike kept saying, "He's a nutter Tony, let's leave him." ... But we didn't and eventually got near Styal entrance ... The one with the little church ... When Len stopped, put his folder like box down that he had and put the eggs in ...

And Len said, "Shush! There are horses there in the field." ... Well me and Mike just giggled, this wassack got excited about horses ... Anyway the horses, for those who know the area, were in the field on the left as you approach the entrance to the woods with the little church on the right ...

Back to the story ... Len said, "Have you ever ridden a horse?" "Nar mate." We said cos we haven't ... He said, "Do you know anything about horses?" ... Again we said "Nar, they're just horses." ... "Don't be

stupid!" He said, which shocked me and Mike ...
"Cheeky little runt! We'll batter him and leave him
here." We whispered to each other ... Me and Mike
that is ....

Len said, "I speak to horses and they listen just as
people do." ... "Nar mate," we said, "They just go nay
and we go nar and they just pull the carts round for
the farmers and that ... It's only cowboys and Injuns
that ride horses really mate." .... "Shush!" He said
again and said, "Wait here and watch this!"....

So he then climbed over the gate leading into the
field, made some strange noises with his hands over
his mouth ... And wow! Guess what? ... Sure enough
one of these horses, a big brown one, came walking
slowly over to Len and when it got close enough he
stroked its head and neck for a while and me and
Mike just stood there, gobs wide open in complete
silence ...

Then Len put his face right up to the horse's nose and
mouth and made more strange noises with his mouth
then led the horse to the gate and climbed on its
back ... "Wow!" We said to each other, "Look at that!"
... And Len said, "Watch this ... this horse will do

anything that I want it to." ...

So our gobs were wide open again, amazed when Len slapped the horse's shoulder and said, "Yo! Yo!"... Then the horse just turned its neck and head round, grabbed Len by the leg and bit him, throwing him off its back to the ground ... At which point a farmer came screaming at us from across the other side of the field, "Get away from those horses you little shits!".....

Then we, Mike and me, pegged it home and left Len the numpty behind .... We never called for him again nor he us ...... And the gang and me just carried on as usual having fun ... and believe me, we never tried mounting real horses ... Our hips worked better eh? Slap! Slap! ... And off we'd trot on us way ....

Hope you enjoyed this story, another one from me childhood memories ......

Oh ... What was your Mam's favourite words she'd say as you went out the door to play? ... Me Mam would yell after me ... "Be home before it gets dark Son." ... Other Mams would say, "Best be in before those street light come on! .... And all us kids would shout back, ... "Ok, I will be."

19

<u>Last trip to Alderley Edge</u>

Hello again .... Ok, it might be a good idea to get yourself a brew and biscuits to dunk .... Right, let's hop on board the old misty memory train and take us a ride back into the past .... This is a pretty strange and long memory to tell ...

One very bright autumn day, a couple of the older gang members called to me house and asked if I was allowed to play out .... And if I was allowed out would I call for some of the other gang members that were about my age because they wanted to try and do something special ....

Me Mam said I had to go to the shops first to get some shopping on tick .... Which I did with no problems ... I came home, gave me Mam her shopping then me Mam said it was ok to play but be home before dark ....

So these older lads, Chris and Colin, not our Colin ... Just sat on the grass verge outside me house waiting while I called for some of the gang members to play out .... Well I returned with about half a dozen lads ...

Then we all set off across our road heading towards the Farmer's Field ... Where we stopped and Chris and Colin explained what their plan was and what they wanted to do .... They explained we were all going to go up to Alderley Edge as they planned to make up some scary things in the caves for the upcoming Hallowe'en weekend ....

"You know," they said, "The kind of stuff you see when you go on the ghost trains at the fairgrounds" ... And the two Kelly brothers, who we hadn't called for yet were going to camp out in the woods by the caves to make sure no one would mess up our scary stuff ....

Well with us was Ayo, Billy, Bryan, Dunny, Ginger, Otto, Mic, Ronnie and me ... The older lads were, Chris, Colin, Frank and the two Kelly brothers ....

We were all sat under the big dead tree awaiting some more of the older ones to join us and bring lots of stuff with them which they did .... They were Jimmy, his brother Bri and Frankie Mez ... But they had brought their girlfriends with them too

Anyway, we all set off carrying between us the stuff the older ones had fetched with them ... including lots of food, water, torches and ropes and booze and cigs ... Now we all went down Ringway Road, cut through by the side of Reynald Chains ... and onto the path at the side of the railway lines ....

That we then followed as we had before to Alderley Edge, getting up to mischief on the way as large groups of kids do ... I think you know what I mean ....

When we got there we all dropped to the floor in the woods for a rest ... After about ten minutes one of the older lads said, "Hey that'll do." ... Pointing at an old dead knotted tree nearby the Blue John shaft ... Which is a round hole in the ground, and pretty deep ....

So then a couple of the older lads wrapped one end of the a rope around the tree ..... Then called over Billy and his little brother Bry and tied the rope on them in turn and lowered them down into the shaft using the tree trunk like a roller if you know what I mean .... Billy and Bry were brave little terriers in the gang ...

Then the heavy bags with the water, food, ropes and torches were lowered down .... Leaving just the bags with the booze, cigs and Halloween stuff up top ... Then they called little Ronnie over and said, "Your turn now." And then lowered him down too ....

But then big Jimmy unwrapped the rope from the knotted tree and just threw it down the shaft and ran off with the other older lads and girls into the woods ... Which left the rest of us younger ones up top wondering what was going on? ....

Believe me, we didn't find what they had done funny one bit .... At first we thought they were just larking around showing off to the girls ... So we waited ... and we waited ...

But after a while we realised they had left us here and weren't coming back ... All we were hearing now was echoing, shouting and crying from us mates down the bottom of the shaft ... By this point we were all really scared and had no idea what to do ....

But then Ayo called out saying, "Look! Look! The rope hasn't fallen all the way down, it's stuck in the mud on the side of the shaft! ... If we tie our shirts together and I get a long thin branch and you lower me down in there a bit, I might be able to get it." ...

So we did what Ayo had suggested and it worked ...
He got the rope by the end nearest the surface and
pulled it out to the top with us pulling him back out of
the hole ..... But believe me it was hard work just
getting Ayo back out just the eight or ten feet or so .....

Well we looped the rope round the tree like the elder
lads had done, tied a bag on the end that we were
going to lower down the hole and away it went down
the shaft to the lads at the bottom ... and asked them to
climb up the rope and out of the shaft, easy peasy ...
Right? .... Wrong!

They just didn't have the strength to climb out of the
shaft ... They took it in turns trying but just couldn't
make it ... They could only seem to climb about 25
feet then just went back down into the darkness of the
shaft ...

So me being a brain box, to the rescue I came .... with
a mint idea ... Shouting down the shaft I said, "Tie the
rope around your waist real good and we'll pull you
up and out." .... Yeah! .... Eeerrr ..... No! ...

We had wrapped the rope around the tree as the big
lads had done but even with the three of us we just

didn't have the strength to pull them out ... So come on everyone help us out and pull this blummin rope with us, Heave! ... Heave! .... Eeerrr .....

What's happened? The rope has come up .... But no one on it ......What the heck? .... So we shout down the hole but no reply .... "Billy you there?" ... Echo ... " Billy, you there?" ... Echo ... "Brian, you there?" ... Echo ... "Brian, you there?" ... Echo ... Lastly, "Ronnie, you there?" All we got back was an echo ... Now we were really worried and was gonna go to the cafe at the entrance to Alderley Edge for help ...

But while we were looking down the shaft for Billy, Brian and Ronnie ... They came running up from behind us shouting, "Here we are ... Here we are." ... Then two men in muddy blue overalls came up to us and said, "Step back away from the shaft .... it's unsafe and your mates are ok." ...

Well here's what had happened ... What we didn't know was this blue shaft as we knew it was the old air shaft for the main cave of Engine Vein and these two men had been down in the cave checking it out for safety reasons and had heard our calls echoing around the cave system below and traced our voices to Brian,

Billy and Ronnie and had led them out through the main cave system behind us ...

Then they took us all to the cafe, got us all a cup of Oxo and toast ... and they had phoned the police to report the incident and when they, the police, arrived it had already gone dark so they took us home in their police vans, asking us kids about what had happened on the way ...

Once home, the police told our parents what had happened ... Then we all got done off our Dads and the big lads and their girlfriends got in trouble off the police ...

We got barred from ever going pot holing again ... Blue shaft got filled in not long after ... No one could ever go down there again ...

Thanks for trying to pull the lads up out of the shaft with us.

20

Saying goodbye to our old friend, The Ring Wood

Eh up! Here's a memory a lot of us older ones and maybe some younger ones too may relate with ... Remember years ago? When we were knee high to grass hoppers?

Most Saturday mornings our Mams and Dads would send us up the road to our local picture house, to watch the Saturday morning mattinee films .... Films like Dan Dare .... Zoro .... Tarzan and Jane .... The Lone Ranger ..... The Three Stooges .... And some great cowboy films .....

Then later, leaving the picture house and on the way home re enacting some of the characters out of the film you had just seen ... And run down the road on your way home slapping your hips thinking and pretending your legs were your trusty old horse .... Bet those memories are coming back now eh? ...

And for me too ... The memories that stand out for me the most were the cowboys and Indians films ....

Now I remember a time, when for a couple of summers, me old pals and me would all gather together at our local dens and make plans about what games we would play or what jobs we could do around our camps .....

Well on this day we decided we needed to find somewhere new so we could build a fort and an Indian encampment, for those who wanted to be cowboys and girls, ... And those who wanted to be Braves and Squaws ...

So then we picked our place ... It was a small wood with a clearing and a small pond and stream running through it known locally as Ring wood ...

Which is very near to the current Manchester Airport Terminal 2 buildings at the top of a road called Hilary Road .... And very near the old lane entrance to Painswick Park, ... With its boating lake back then ... Just to give you a rough idea of where we were ...

Anyway we're off now, slapping us hips as we crossed the first road, Woodhouse Lane really ... Riding by the houses to our left then through the bushes by the flats, across the stream, then over the field and into Ring

Wood ....

Where we formed groups to gather and collect the things we would need .... Like old corrugated sheets from the old buildings from the past, old branches, long straight sticks and as much grass as we could find .... We put it in piles under instruction from our captain, a lad named Malcolm Sargent ... Aptly named ... but it was his real name ...

We built us selves a fort... It was a mess really but we thought it was great ... A little den with sticks for a roof and then covered in grass, a load of old broken bushes and sticks as the fort walls and a circle of stones in the middle for us fire .... This took us a while over a few days to build ....

And then we got an old school book with blank pages in it and made a register of the troop ... Boys first as it was back then ...

Malc Sargent the Captain, Irish Mick the chief scout, in charge of weapons was little Ronnie, food and drinks storeman Eddy, truce maker Arthur ... Who is still me best mate after sixty years ... and the tower watchmen were Mike and Malc .... They were the best tree climbers we had .... Steve, me younger brother and me ...

I can't remember what we were supposed to be, and it doesn't say in me diary ha ha ha ....

Then there was the girls ... Pauline the cook ... Maureen the cleaner ... Ruth the store girl, in charge of the girl's things ... and the other girls were Linda white hair, Linda song bird, Margaret little rabbit, and me sister Pam was panther ...

Don't think I got a top memory, these kids names were written in me diary I kept at the time and still have ...

Now for the Indians ... There was Dave, his brother Ayo, Brian and his brother Alan, then Jimmy, Danny and Jamaican Syd .....

Anyway back to the memories ... We had this top fort in the woods and the Injuns had their camp out in the field ....

So all you had all summer long was a load of kids acting out what we had seen on the movie screens at the A.B.C Northenden that week as I'm sure you did too ... Running round slapping the living daylights out of your legs and having fun as kids ...

And each day when allowed out we would go to our fort, den or Indian camp and play our games ... Climb trees, make toast on the fire, drink your council pop, water out of your bottle ... Well we really made a top place for us kids to play in over a couple of years ....

Till the sad day one summer when we met up as usual, cut across the field at the back of the flats only to find a very high fence across where we would usually go down by the side of the small pond where the stream led ....

Only to find a couple of men by the large high fence stood on our path who told us we weren't allowed in the woods anymore and to go back home ... Or they would get the police as it's private land and they were going to extend the airport buildings and put a new road across there and that it was dangerous ....

So off home we all went slapping us legs but not with the same enthusiasm as before ...

A few nights later a couple of the older kids went to where our fort and camp had been to retrieve some of their things and ours but to no avail ... The camp and fort had been flattened and removed but the wood and pond had not been touched ...

Well they did extend the buildings and built a hotel there called The Excelsior and a road leading up to it .... But that was years later and they put fancy flags on poles alongside the new road ...

When me and me Sara got married I went back there with Sara and told her some of the stories from my childhood times spent in that place ...

One of the young lads I didn't name died during the second summer holidays from an asthma attack ... I'll just tell you for respect his name was Paul and he lived on Woodhouse Lane near the tree where I met my late wife Barbara (But that's another story for another time) ...

And one of the young girls not mentioned was killed by a hit and run driver on Styal Road, her name was Lillian .....

Hope me memory helps you to relive your childhood days too ... And maybe, just maybe, you can tell your kids or grandkids about some of your childhood adventure days eh? ,,,

And if any of the old gang are still out there ... I know me old mate Arthur and a couple of the others are too ... Just hope that you too can relive this memory with me ...

And trust you're still making lots of good memories today and hope they won't be buried under tar and cement like our old friend The Ring Wood was.

21

<u>The swan lake of our childhood</u>

Hello again ... Trust you're well and are ready to take another trip with me on me old memory train down memory lane... Here is another one for you ...

I'll start by explaining where this memory took place ... Ok, where the Virgin Media buildings are now on Simonsway in Wythenshawe there used to be a pretty large figure of eight pond situated in the big field between Hatchett Woods and Shadow Woods .... And it was a pretty deep body of water ... We local kids nick named it The Swans ... I don't know why it was called this ...

Anyway here's the story ... Now I'm not sure of the day this all took place but I think it was a Saturday ... And it was a freezing cold start to the day and I gets a knock on me front door and I answer it ... It's a couple of me pals calling for me to play out as usual ...

And they asked if I would be able to go to Shadow Wood to fix up our den and make it more weather proof so the roof didn't leak and protect our goodies that we had stored in there, but bring our scout knives, saw and axe back home to clean and store at home over this cold and damp weather so they wouldn't get rusty or stolen ...

So I shouted back into the house, "Dad ... Dad ... is it ok for me to play out please?" ... I always had to say please and thank you when me Dad was about as he was pretty strict and hated bad manners ... Well me Dad said. "Ok, but stay out of trouble and make sure your back in here before dark." ...

Well off we went ... Down Ravenscar Crescent onto Cornishway, down Portway, then cut over the green facing St. Anthony's church and on to Prinknash Road .... And started calling for us mates that lived round there ...

First off was Mike, then Jack, then me bestest mate Arthur, then Linda who lived in the end house next to the woods ... And some other pals that lived on Prinknash Road and Hatchett Road came along too.

There was about ten of us by now, and the other part of our gang, about six more, who had said they would meet us there ...

Anyway down Prinknash Road, onto Hatchett Road and into the woods by the small pond we went ... Cut through Hatchett Woods and onto the field to meet the rest of the gang there ...

But as we approached The Swans, the lake that is, there was a lot of shouting and screaming from a very large group of kids on our side of the lake ... They weren't all our mates so we thought there was a gang fight and ran over to help our guys ...

But as we got closer we could see so many kids around the edge of the lake and some other kids making their way across the lake on sticks, branches and all sorts of stuff ...

It was then I realised the lake was frozen over and some kids had gone through the ice near the middle and the kids going across the ice were trying to help to get them out of the water ....

Everyone was barking at each other with ideas and were frantically getting whatever they could out of the woods and field to make a pathway across the ice .... It was real bedlam ...

There had been a home made raft on the lake ...
Which I think the kids in trouble had been trying to
drag across the ice ... I don't know ...

Suddenly there was Danny, one of our gang with what
I thought was rags ... He had this kid who was just
limp, not moving at all, over his shoulder ... All the
kids were celebrating 'cept those still at and in the
water ...

Then Patrick, Danny's brother, appeared through the
sea of kids, with the other kid that had been trapped in
the water over his shoulder ... But this time
immediately there were adult hands grabbing the kid
off Patrick and other adults were shifting us kids away
from the water ...

These adults turned out to be the police and the fire
brigade ... I don't know who had got them but they
were there and made all us kids go home ...

At the night time the police came to me house, as they
did all of our houses to ask us what we had seen and
what we knew ... One of the kids that had gone
through the ice had apparently died but thankfully the
other kid had survived but was in a bad way ...

Well this is where, for me, me childhood days started to come to an end, cos after this none of us kids were allowed anywhere near those woods or fields and our Mums or Dads now kept a much closer eye on us kids so really we all just started to drift apart and never again would the gang be the same ...

The lake got filled in, the field and woods were fenced off, and someone put Highland cattle on there where we used to play ...

The following summer the older kids started dating .... Us younger ones just played out with local kids till we were much older ourselves ....

Patrick was awarded some special medal off the police and fire brigade .... We all just grew up and grew apart and only a few of us kept in touch ... But even then things would happen that none of us pals could ever have foreseen ...

I can't but wonder how we would have all grown up if these events hadn't happened, or we hadn't been there and witnessed them? ... What and where else would we be now? ...

We all got to realise just how dangerous water can be ... Especially frozen over lakes, ponds or canals ...

I think we all know about someone or have read about someone local to you losing their life whilst just trying to have a bit of fun skating on the ice ... How sad

Thank you for coming back with me on the old misty memory train down memory lane and reliving this sad and tragic memory with me

22

<u>Our building projects...bikes and bogeys</u>

Come on in folks, chillout .... So just kick off your shoes, get a brew, relax and let's step through the fog of time back to our childhood .....

This memory starts in Moss Side and Fallowfield ... After walking down the long path along the side of Princess Road passed Southern Cemetery and beyond I ended up just outside the bus depot in Moss Side when I saw an old pal named Johnny Gee who worked in the Wycliffe picture house a bit futher down the road on the right ....

So I called over to him, "Hey Johnny, how's things?" He waved and crossed over the road from the Alexandra Park side ... And said, "Hey mate!" to me .... Then said, "Yeah man, not too bad here, how's it with you?" .... So I just said, "Yeah all sweet .... just on me way to see our Colin to finish off making a bike up from old bits we have gathered together." ...

Our Colin and me ... Our Colin by the way was me

Dad's youngest brother but was only three years older than me .... and was more like a brother to me rather than an uncle ...

Anyway Johnny said, "I'm going to work now and if you want to watch a film for free just tap on the side door and I'll let you in so you can see the film for free." .... At the time I think the film was Blue Hawaii with Elvis Presley ... Anyway we parted company ... I said, "Ta-ra .. See ya later gayter." ... He walked off down Princess Road to work at the Wycliffe and I cut down the side streets to meet our Colin at a second hand shop where he helped out at the weekends and stored the bike parts in the yard ....

Well we met up, went in the yard and finished off building us bike ... Putting some finishing touches to the bike before we were going to paint it ... His boss, I never knew his name, said, "Have you two finished the bike yet as I have a customer looking to buy a bike and I ain't got one?" .... Colin said, "We ain't done yet and we ain't painted it either." ...

His boss disappeared for a few minutes ... Then came back and said, "Is it rideable?" ... We said, "Yeah but there's no front brake." .... His boss disappeared again then came back and said, "Will you take ten bob for it?" .... "What as it is?" We said ... And he said, "Yeah, but I want a cut." .... Well ten bob back then was a fortune to us kids, so we let Colin's boss do the deal and that was that .....

After this we had no project to do so our Colin went home to me Ninny Ratcliff's round the corner and I went down to the Wycliffe picture house to see Johnny and watch a free film ... Yeah! ... And all this dosh in me pocket! ... Three and sixpence was my cut so I was well chuffed ....

Well I got to the Wycliffe and knocked on the side door ... Johnny let me in and Jimmy is over there, another mate from round the corner from where I lived back in Wythenshawe .... The film was half way through and with me bragging about me money and how I got it .... I missed most of the film ...

At the end we just walked out of the place like everyone else ... I said, "Ta-ra." to Johnny and we, Jimmy and me, got the 103 bus back home to Wythenshawe ...

Well this memory ends really with the point of the

story ... The following weekend our Colin called up to see me on another bike he had made ... This was a really great bike with gears and everything ... It even had mud guards ... So I had a go at riding it with our Colin sat on the cross bar ...

We hadn't gone far when a policeman said, "Hey you two, stop I want a word." ... Well we stopped and he came over and took our names and addresses and told us we shouldn't be riding two on a bike nor be riding on the pavements ... Then he just told us to go home and don't do it again ...

So off we went walking home, pushing the bike... Then when we got home to our house we started a new project of making a bogey ...

We thought no more of the police incident, Colin just told me the man who had bought our bike the week before was a pop star ... A lead singer of a famous pop band who had flown into Manchester Airport, hired a car to go to some television studios in Manchester to do a live show and the hire car had broken down and the rest of his band had travelled by road separately with their gear in a van .....

We never saw this singer who bought our bike ... So
I've not got a clue who he was or where he had
been .... But it just goes to show we are all at the
mercy of fate eh? .... Don't know why that singer dint
get a taxi or bus though ... Our Colin always thought it
was the lead singer out of The Drifters, I don't know
why ...

Oh we heard from that policeman ... We were taken to
court and fined £2.00 each for riding two on a bike ...
Hope you like my little memory ... This happened in
the summer holidays of 1961 ... A long time ago
now .....

Did you ever get pulled up by the local bobby for
riding two on a bike or for riding on the pavement? ...
Or maybe we were just unlucky.

23

<u>The shock of growing up</u>

Well hello again .... Trust you're well and your day has treated you kindly .... Earlier today me wife Sara was finishing off sorting out all me old bits of diaries and notes out of the case in the loft ... And she brought them down for me to go through them with her, to decide which bits to re-type out and keep and which were too far gone to read ...

Well there was this old lined school exercise book which had been re-covered in old brown paper ... You know the sort, we all had them back in the day, remember ... We all covered our school books like this back in the late fifties and the early sixties ...

Written on the front was a line which read ... I thought she was dying ... So being nosey and not remembering what this book was ... I opened it up and though the writing was very poor, I never was a tidy or neat writer and the words were faded, I read what it said inside ... Within a few lines I remembered the day ... Do you want me to tell you what it read? .... Ok then, grab a brew and sit thee down cos here we go again down the old misty memory lane ...

It read today, Saturday, Eddy and Joe called for me to play out with them and go and call for a couple of new mates they had made in school ... These mates lived over in a new territory called Crossacres .... Where there's a large wood that has a stream running through it and is at the side of Crossacres Road ....

So as always off we galloped ... You know the score by now eh? ... Slappin' us thighs and making horse noises with our mouths .... believing we were riding a horse ... C'mon join in, slap ya hips .... Now we're trotting along it shouldn't take us to long to get there ...

Well we're here now at the first of our new mate's houses ... It was on Meladin Crescent and we knocked on the door ... A boy named Mike answered the door ... Yep, he was one of the two mates we were looking for and Mike had two sisters that were older than him by about a year or so I reckon .... They wanted to join our gang as did their brother Mike ...

Anyway Mike shouted back into the house, "Mam is it

ok for us all to play out?" .... Mike's Mam shouted
back, "Well where are you all going?" ... "Just in the
woods Mam." Mike replied, "The ones at the back of
the house Mam." ... His Mam shouted, "Right but be
home in time for your tea then." ... "Right Mam."
Mike said ... "We will." ....

I can't spell the horse noises we made with us lips but
I'm sure you know which ones I mean eh? .... Then
slapped us hips and away we trotted again down
Meladin Crescent ... I can see you slappin' your hips
and making the old noises with me ... See you ain't
forgot have you? ....

Then we all stopped at the corner house where this
other new friend lived called Pete .... We knocked on
his door and he just came out and said, "Where we all
off to then? C'mon." ... So off we all trotted back
down Meladin Crescent onto Brownley Road, turned
right and straight away there's an entrance into the
woods where we went in ... A couple of Mike and
Pete's mates that I don't know the names of met us in
the woods and wanted to play with us too so now we
had us a bit of a gang ...

After going just a few yards into the woods down the

path we made a little den and a clearing and then sat down chatting about what game we were going to play ...

We decided to play cowboys and Indians ... The cowboys on one side and the Indians on the other .... Then off we went ... We were the Indians on this day and the others were cavalry and their wives ... Well we made us dens and then decided to attack the fort that the cavalry had made .... They were still building their fort at this point ... And we just threw these pretty straight branches we had found and stripped of their bark ... and used them as arrows and spears ....

But within minutes of our game starting a shout came out from the cavalry ... Ballies! Ballies! Ballies! ... You older ones out there know what this means .... It means stop, we give in ..... So we stopped and gathered round praising each other for winning the battle so easily ...

When Mike said, "We need to get her home fast, she's dying ... she's dying!" ... And one of Mike's sisters was trembling and crying saying, "I'm going to die ain't I ..... I'm going to die!" .... Well we all crapped it ... She had blood, real blood, not pretending, runnning down her legs ... So we thought one of our spears had stabbed her good and proper ...

So along with Mike, we all got the girls home, especially the one that was bleeding .... Us lads that were Indians were all blaming each other and really thought she was going to die .... I think you girls out there know what had really happened ... Us lads are a bit slower realising these things eh? .... After this we never let too many girls in the gang ... And our horse noises and leg slapping days were numbered ....

Why do these things happen the way they do? ... They just stole away our childhood innocence ......

I didn't name all our old gang members as I'm sure you'll know who they are from me previous stories ... And it would be embarrassing for the girl concerned for me to have named her

Hope you enjoyed joining me on me journeys going back through the mists of time on our good old memory train .... Thank you for reading this funny yet scary story from my childhood years.

24

Our last Hallowe'en as a gang..and the hailstones

E bar gum ... This crazy rain and wind of late autumn reminds me of an evening ...

A Hallowe'en evening that is ... When some of the older gang members were planning a night out in the Moss wood ... There was Tic and Dan, Jimmy and Bry, Barry, Chris and Colin, not our colin, and some girls older than us ... Led by Ruth and Brenda ... There was Maureen, Margaret, Linda, and Karen ...Then me, Arthur, little Ronnie and Billy ....We were the youngest lads there ...

Well we had all spent earlier that day cutting out us swedes and cut faces on them ... Well some of these older lads had nicked some candles from a local church to put in the swedes to light them up like lanterns ... Oh yeah .... The reason we used swedes even though they're a sod to hollow out is that us Mams would use the waste swede for us dinner the next day ...

Well me, Arthur, Ronnie and Billy asked us Mams if we could go with these older kids to play out for the Hallowe'en night and they said, "Go on sod off, but don't be too late home ... So off we all went with us swedes in hand to the Moss Wood, which I have metioned in the memories I've already shared with you .....

Well we trudged over the Farmer's field, passed the old abandoned original Moss Nook School on Ringway Road (Not the new Moss Nook School, that was on Portway.), then down by the side of the old chicken coups to the Moss Wood ...

But this year was different as the field by the chicken coups had been ploughed and raked flat .... Other years the old man that owned this land would just plough small parts about ten yards square and plant things like spring onions, lettuce or spuds ... Not this year though .....

Anyway back to the story ... I hope you're not getting lost? ... We got to the Moss Wood where we all collected some wood and swiftly made a pretty big camp fire and lit it as it was pretty cold that night ....

Well it was a pretty big full moon as I recall and you could see the bats flying passed the big bright moon .... And somewhere outside the fire light you could hear a solitary owl tooting his head off .....

Well then the bigger boys took their coats off and laid them on the floor around the fire and had gotten sticks, stuck them in the ground next to their coats and hung their now lighted swede lanterns on them ....

And sat on the coats on the ground with their girlfriends and started... well, you know, that kisses stuff ... For me, Billy, Arthur and Ronnie this was yuk yuk at the time .... and was for sisses ...

So we wandered over to where there is a small mud bank under some trees and hung our swedes up in the trees with the lit candles inside .... and just listened to the owl tooting his head off and the girls giggling ...

Then I think it was Tic who said, "Listen you lot, I got a ghost story to tell ... Do you wanna hear it or what?" ... So all the big uns said, "Yeah, go on, go on then." ..... So Tic said "You know about the haunted Egyptian mummies in the pyramids that you see in films don't you?" .... We all said, "Yeah go on!" ... So

Tic said, "Well ..." .....

Just as he said, "Well ..." ... There was a huge crash, bang and flash of lightning ... We couldn't see the moon now, as the sky seemed really black, full of clouds, and it got really cold and windy ...... Then there was another flash of lightning and bang at the same time ....

So you can imagine can't you ... We and even all the big uns were scared sssshhhh ... less and grabbed us coats but before we could really do anything or go anywhere the sky just dropped on us the biggest and baddest hailstones we've ever seen ....

We all just ran as fast as we could back over the ploughed field by the chicken coups, then over Ringway Road, through the old Farmer's field, back onto the housing estate and home to our houses ...

Not sure about the big uns, but me and Billy, who lived across the road, ran straight into me house where our Mams and Dads were waiting as we had been a lot longer than we thought .... and we were late home ... And yeah we had got soaking wet and full of mud from the ploughed field ...

And the worst was yet to come .... Billy's Mam and Dad took him home and me Dad took me into the back room and ..... well gave me butt a good taste of his leather belt ... For being late home, ruining me clothes and somehow he had found out about the candles so I got an extra whooping for being with people who had stolen candles from a church ..... Me butt was sure very hot that night eh? ....

Anyway, tragedy and death would strike some members of the gang a few weeks later ...

Word spread around the gang that Ruth was pregnant and the Dad was Colin ... And over the next couple of weeks they were making plans to get married, with their parents consent ... Sadly, somehow Ruth lost the baby and their parents thought it best if they stayed apart now and didn't get married as they were still pretty young ...

But no one could keep them apart and they ran away from home together ... They ran off to Turret Wood and lived in a tent for a couple of weeks there ... During this time, both boys and girls from the gang were taking them supplies up each day ... Including some dimps, which we got from ashtrays at home and from the floor of phone boxes in our area, for Colin to break up and make roll ups with as he was a smoker ... But somehow the police tracked them down and took them home ...

A couple of days later word got out that Ruth had taken an overdose and commited suicide in the bath ... Why in the bath I don't know, maybe so her parents didn't walk in on her while she was doing the deed ... The heartbreak didn't end there as a couple of days later Colin's Dad found Colin hanging from a tree in their back garden ...

It was so poignant that both Ruth and Colin's funerals were on the same day in the week leading up to Christmas ... As the hearses and cars passed our houses, everyone bowed their heads and touched their collars as a mark of respect ... This was terrible for the gang and must have been so much worse and heartbreaking for their own families ...

This tragedy, and other events, marked the beginning of the end of our gang as shortly after this, the large gang began to splinter in to smaller groups ...

And the older ones formed couples with the ones they

fancied and were more interested in what boys and girls do when they're let .,.. Including boozing, dancing, clubbing it down in Manchester city centre and riding motor bikes or scooters ...

And they became mods or rockers, racing up and down the lanes between the fields and the woods we had not long ago spent our childhood days in .... Oh how time flies eh? ...

And these days, most of our old play areas, are no where to be seen, eeeee bar gum how sad?

25

__The abrupt ending of my childhood__

Arh this trip down the old misty memory lane is a
very sad, heartbreaking one as it's where me
childhood came to a sudden crashing end ...

One autumn afternoon me, Arthur, Billy, Noel Lan,
Ronnie and a few other pals called over to a friend's
house to ask if he was playing out ... Anyway we
knocked on his door several times but got no reply ...
Then just as we were about to leave Billy grabbed a
small transistor radio off little Ronnie that he had been
given off his Dad for his birthday, which really upset
Ronnie, so I told Billy to give it back ... Billy said,
"No." ...

One word led to another and a fight started between
us ... Then there were fists flying everywhere ... And
we wrestled, which caused us both to fall over against
the door ... We heard a loud crack and the little
window in the front door of our friend's house had
been cracked ... So as kids do, we all ran off home so
as not to get the blame and thought no more about it ...

Until the police came to me house later that night .... With a stern voice the policeman told me Dad he wanted a word with me down the station. Then off we went but when we got to the police station ..... There to my surprise, was Billy, Arthur and their Dads, They were already there ...

Well to cut things short, what we were at the police station for was our friend that we had called for earlier was in the house when we called ... And when his Dad had got home from work his Dad had gone mad about the cracked window ... So our so called friend told his Dad we had tried to break into their house ...

Looking back, we think this lie was told so our friend's Dad could claim the money off their house insurance, as we had no money to pay for the cracked window ... (Arthur, Billy or me) ... We had already explained to our Dads what had happened and our Dads had said to the police, "C'mon, they're just kids and it's an accident so we ain't paying for no window."

That's when for us tragedy struck ... As the police then cautioned us and charged us all with attempted burgalry ... And arranged a court appearance date for us to appear before the courts ...

Anyway, when we appeared before the judges there were three of them as this was the magistrates court at Minshull Street ... All the things we had ever been in court for were brought up and used against us ... Like riding two on a bike (£2.00 fine), trespass (£2.00 fine), and apple scrumping ... Where we also had gone into the potting shed at the orchard and got caught in the shed. Which meant we were charged with office breaking and the theft of apples ... Which we got 90 days custodial sentence for, which we served in Rose Hill remand centre for boys ...... Followed by a two years probation order, which we were serving at the time of our arrest for the cracked window ...

So then both me and Arthur were sentenced to three years approved school ... Arthur was sent to Mobberley and I was sent to St. Joseph's in Nantwich, near Crewe in Cheshire ...

Sadly within a week of being in St. Joseph's I was sexually abused by two of the monks in the press shop. Where they, the monks, were supposed to be teaching me how to set type prints and operate a small printing press ... The tall monk grabbed me by me hair, then me arms and dragged me face down over a work bench ... While the smaller, fat monk did the deed on my side of the work bench, nuf said on that ....

Then as they were laughing and bragging and I pulled my shorts up ... I noticed the door to the printing room was slightly open ... So that's when I made a run for the door ... The next thing I remember was running accross some road and onto a field where there was a canal ... There was a clump of bushes by the canal and that's where I hid ...

A few hours later it was going dark so I followed the canal till I came to a road bridge and it had a road sign on it saying Manchester Airport and an arrow pointing the way ... So off I went following road signs heading home to Wythenshawe where Manchester Airport lies ...

The journey home took me about three days and nights, but I made it ... I ended up at the back of Manchester Airport, near the fields and woods I'd played in with me pals just weeks earlier ... As an innocent child .... But right now I was cold, tired, hungry, thirsty and very dirty, wondering what the hell had happened to me ...

Well me childhood days were now over but the skills I had learned like scavenging food from the swill at local pig farms and taking the odd couple of chickens eggs and building a shelter would all now come in handy and keep me alive ...

But first I needed water, so I got meself down to the River Bollin ... Where I had meself a real good, much needed drink of water by cupping me hands and drinking the water ... Then it was over to the pig and chicken farms just off Styal Road and make a den in a local barn under the bales of hay ... Once I had done this then the rest now was child's play as they say?

Each evening time for the next week or so, would be garden hopping and borrowing nights ... That means you go in gardens one at a time, checking on the washing lines to see whats been left out to dry overnight, This works great in the summer months ...

Anyway you find articles of clothing that should fit you ... So you'd borrow socks and undies off one line ... another garden, another line, vest and shirt ... another line, trousers and jumpers, I think you get the idea ... Also at these rich people's houses over near Heald Green there were always shoes, adult's and children's, left outside the back doors overnight ... Maybe rich folk put slippers on when they go indoors, who knows? ...

It took a while but now I was well set up. Food and drinks off the farms, a bit of shop lifting for things like soap, a comb and a magnifying glass to start fires with ... The fire was to cook eggs and other food stuffs ... This, along with the borrowed clobber off the washing lines, kept me going ...

Then one morning while I was out and about cutting through Shadow Wood, who should I bump into? Yep, you got it, me old pal Arthur ... Who had also absconded from his approved school in Mobberley a few weeks earlier ... Wow, we were both so shocked at meeting up ...

Then Arthur told me his friend had been putting him up in their loft without his parents knowing. But we both agreed it would be better for us both to stay together and live at me main base in the barn ... Yippee, company at last. Now then together we made a fantastic unbeatable team ...

We drank half a cup each of cream every morning

which the farmers left in their milk churns at the end of their lanes ... We had even got a part time job sorting tomatoes out at Matthews' Tomatoes greenhouses on Styal Road, which put much needed money in our pockets .... What could possibly go wrong for us now? ...

I'll tell you what, very early one morning we were both awakened by loud barking and growling of police dogs and police all over the barn where we lived under the bales of hay .... That was that ... We were arrested and sent back to our respective approved schools ... Arthur back to Mobberley and me back to St. Joseph's ...

Where within days I was raped by the same two monks but this time there was a wooden mallet on the bench which I belted one of the monks over the head with and ran out of the building, down the drive and onto the main road where I flagged down a truck ...

I got inside and we drove off. While travelling down the road the driver, a young Scottish sounding man, asked, "What the hell was you running from? Just look at the state of you." ... I Begged him, "Please don't take me back mister, please don't take me back." ... He said, "Look, my name is John but I can't help you if I don't know what's going on." As these words left his mouth he pulled the truck over onto a small car park at the side of a small transport cafe. Then pulled up and asked me to get out the truck but leave the door open while I told him what had gone on. So I agreed ...

I stood at the side of the truck with the passenger side door opened ... Then blurted it all out that I had run out of the approved school ... He said, "Ok ... ok ... that makes two of us." Well, whilst traveling down the roads he explained he too had run away from approved school a few years earlier and that he was still on the run ...

He then told me, "Look lad, I live in Glasgow ... You're very welecome to come and stay with me for while if you like." .... Then told me his story, which is his business and not for me to repeat, except to tell you he had run away from his approved school in Scotland ... Slept in a cemetery, woke up the next morning next to a head stone ... and the person on the head stone had been born a year before him and died at about the age of seven ...

Now he said he had then got a job at the docks in Glasgow as a dock hand using that name and date of birth on the grave stone ... Maybe I could try and do the same thing .... How John had become a driver I never got to know ...

Anyway I moved in with John ... He lived in a small bedsit on Medwyn Street in the heart of Glasgow ... Anyway though I kept on trying I just could not get a job on the docks or anywhere else ... and John was out all day doing his job driving ... So our friendship began to wane after a couple of months as he was paying for everything and I was paying for nothing. He asked me to leave, Which I did ...

I had arrived at his home with nothing 'cept the clothes on my back, and left the same way, but with better clothes on that John had bought me ... Now came the hard part, getting back to good old Manchester by walking and thumbing lifts which I did

Once home back at me Mam and Dad's, me Dad made a few phone calls to probation officers, solicitors and others to get advice on what he should do with me ... Well all the best advice was the same me Dad said, and that was to get a solicitor and probation officer and go along wth them and me Dad and hand myself in ...

Which I did, but I never mentioned John, I told them all I had just been living off the land ... And when asked why I had absconded and attacked the monk with a mallet I told them the truth ... Their answer was amazing ..... "Now, NOW," They said, "The less said about this kind of thing the better ... These are righteous men of the cloth you're talking about you know? You'll only get yourself in deeper trouble than you're already in." ...

Now I was arrested and sent to Risley remand prison near Warrington for a few months, then sent to a classifying unit for a few weeks, then transferred to the closed unit high security for three months ...

Then one morning out of the blue I was transferred again to a borstal in Northamptonshire where I stayed till I was released in February 1968 ....

Oh, and guess who the first person apart from family was that I bumped into at a local bus stop just after I came home? ... Yep yer right me old bestest pal Arthur.

26
Homeward bound

Well hello again ... Just a another memory of mine for you to digest ...

This story really starts like this ... As it's the very strange story of how I got home after leaving me friend John and his Medwyn Street bed sit in Glasgow

I won't take you round the houses, I failed to get a job and couldn't afford to go half on the bills at John's place ... And I had borrowed some money off him for various things I needed to see me through while hoping to get a job and pay him back ...

But no job meant I had no way I could pay the money back I owed him ... So basically he threw me out on me butt ... Just me and the clothes I was wearing ...

So being a lad about the town, so I thought ... It shouldn't be too hard to get back home to Manchester ... So off I went and headed back towards Manchester on Shank's pony and tried to thumb any lift going me way ... And at night just sleeping rough in the country side as on the first day I had been given

149

a lift out of the city .... But not had any other lift since ...

Well, I had been on the road now for about five days and nights with no food and had been drinking water out of cattle troughs ... I sat down with me back against a stone field wall, rather weak and very tired ... and fell asleep ...

I was awakened by a car horn beeping as it went passed me and it was now beginning to snow ... I looked around me to see if I could see any type of farm buildings where I could maybe shelter for the night, but there was none to be seen .... I knew if I fell back asleep where I was I would freeze to death ...

So I turned back around from the field wall, ready to start walking ... To the sight of a man's face in front of me who said simply, "Sit down, you'll no get far in this me lad ... I'll help you ... You cannot go any further, especially in this snow." ... Which by now was really falling heavily with big flakes ...

So I sat down ... more like fell down ... and this man climbed over the wall ... Then after a couple of minutes he climbed back to me side of the wall near the road and said, "You need to climb over the wall with me ... Don't worry I'll help you." ... So we both climbed over the wall to where he had made like a tunnel shape shelter and he said, "Come on let's get in." ... Which I did and so did he .... And again I fell asleep ...

The next morning I awoke to him saying, "Come on, you must eat." ... And he gave me two boiled eggs and a whole white cooked fillet of fish which I whoofed down as I was so hungry ... Then he gave me a drink of water out of a bottle ...

I said, "Thank you, but who are you and how can I repay you for your kindness?" ... He said, "Well .... you can carry my sack." ... Which all his shelter stuff had been stashed in to ... And I agreed ...

The snow had stopped now but it was freezing cold and the crisp snow on the ground was about three inches deep ... And we both just walked, me carrying his sack after he had loaded the sleeping stuff back into it and he just walked in front silently ...

After a few more miles of walking the snow returned again and just as before we climbed over a field wall, set up the shelter, we both got in and fell asleep again ...

Next morning, again he fed me with two boiled eggs and a whole white fish fillet and gave me a drink of water out of a glass bottle ... Then we packed away the sleeping gear and I climbed over the wall to the road side with his sack ....

And then he said, "Pass me my sack back please, there is something I want."... So I passed the sack back to him ... He was still in the field by the wall .... Then he simply said, "Here's your lift, flag him down." ... So I turned around and sure enough there was a small truck coming down the road ...

So I flagged him down ... He stopped ... and asked, "Where you heading son?" ... So I told him, "Home to Manchester." ... And he said, "C'mon then get in." ... So I called out to me friend over the wall, "Yeah it's a lift and he's .... " .... There was no one there .... No sack, no nothing .... So I said to the man in the truck, "Did you see me friend, or see where he went?" ... He simply replied, "No Son, there's only you here." ... I had another quick look round but no one was anywhere to be seen

So I climbed up into this little truck and settled down in the seat ... This little truck and its driver gave me a lift all the way back to Manchester without speaking very much at all and dropped me off at the gates of Alexandra Park, Princess Road in Moss Side and he said, "You'll have to get out here Son." ...

It wasn't too far from where me Gran Annie, my Dad's Mum lived ... So I got out of the truck and said, "Thank you." ... And off he drove and I went straight to me Gran's house, where I got cleaned up and borrowed some of our Colin's clothes ...

I told me Gran the whole story and me Gran simply said, "It must have been an angel ... But you need to get back home to your Dad's now and hand yourself in to the police." ... To this day I don't know what it, or who, he was who saved me from the snow and fed me and gave me shelter ... Nor do I know who the driver of the truck was as he hardly said a word ... But what I do know is my life had been saved by that stranger walking with me and by that mysterious truck driver ...

I did go home to me Dad's and handed meself in to a probation officer called Mr Warrell, who accompanied me to Brownley Road police station where I was kept over night till being taken to court the next day where I was re-committed for three years and sent to Risley, near Warrington, where I was kept for six months before being transferred to a classifying unit ... Then from there to a closed unit and finally on to borstal to serve my sentence ... Then go home at last

Hope you like this strange and unexplained episode in me life

Just my thoughts

I often wonder how many other people have had strange unexplainable things happen to them .... And just like me mainly kept it to yourself as you were scared of ridicule and laughter? ...

A lot of people believe in U.F.Os .... Aliens ... The flat earth ... The hollow earth .... Haunted places and ghosts .... Angels .... Bigfoot... The lock Ness Monster.... and so on ... And many say they have seen these things .....

I wonder if they are just telling the truth and it's the doubtful majority who just can't see the wood for the trees ..... I wonder what your thoughts are on these strange and unexplainable events that go on all around us each day? ...

To be honest I have had a lot of strange and unexplainable things happen to and around me and many times I have been with a good few people who witnessed and experienced the same things ....

Some of these stories I hope to tell you in my next book, The sky is my witness .. It saw it all ... Hope you can join me .. Till then take care, see thee friend

27

<u>WHO NICKED ME CHILDHOOD?</u>

Who nicked me childhood? ... As it seems one day I was out playing with all me pals having so much fun and laughter with not a worry or care in the world ...

Then I fell asleep in the local park and had a nightmare where all me fun had been stolen by some strange event called growing up .....

In this nightmare I was hauled out of bed at an ungodly hour and told I had to go to work and earn some cash ....

As someone has to pay the bills like rent, gas, water, electricity, council tax .... Then on top of that I would need more money to pay for me food, clothes, pots, pans, plates, cups, knives, forks, spoons. bedding, curtains, carpets, furniture, including a bed, three piece suite, washing machine, fridge, cooker, a table to eat at ...

OH, and I would have to wash me own dirty clothes, cook me own food, clean me own house, and even decorate the place ... Buy light bulbs, lamp shades, a clock ... And who's gonna pay for me game console and games? ... And what about when I need a shower? ... A towel, soap, shampoo, hair gel, toothpaste, comb, toilet roll? ...

PHEW! ... Glad it was just a bad dream eh? ... EH ... Whooor! ... Someone please wake me up, I want me childhood back! Someone, please Maaaaaaaam! .... Where are you? ... Wake me up please ... I want me childhood days of fun back ... Maaaaaaam.

WHO NICKED ME CHILDHOOD? ...... SOMEONE PLEASE, ... PLEASE WAKE ME UP! .... PRETTY PLEASE! ..... HE EEE ELP! ... MUM WHERE ARE YOU? ..... PLEASE HELP ... MUUUUUM!

28

The Giddy up gang

One very hot Easter weekend in the late Fifties, me and a few of me pals were out in the local fields near our houses ... We were just lay on our backs, hands behind us heads taking in the sunshine and chatting when ......

Whoooooosh! A jet fighter flew very low over the field where we lay ... Well talk about pooing us pants ... Though we all lived very close to Manchester Airport we had never seen nor heard a jet fighter before and wondered what it was ...

Now we were all stood up and shaking a little, we decided to play a game of cowboys goodies and baddies ... So we split up into two groups, the outlaws on one side and the Sheriff and his men on the other side ...

Then slappin' us hips and saying giddy up, we went to opposite sides of the field to make us plans on what we would do in the game ... We had Danny Lynch on our side directing us in what to do and say ... We were the outlaws ...

So Danny went over to the Sheriff's group and told them our plans of robbing the bank and running off with the money ... And how they, the Sheriff's men, would catch and kill us all at the end of the game by the old dead tree at the side of the field ...

I don't know how many of you remember how the games we played were planned out before we started ...

Anyway the game went great till the end ... When we were all killed and laying on the floor and the Sheriff and his men rode off slapping their hips into the sunset ... When suddenly one of the lads screamed out and just fell to the ground rolling over in pain ...

Wow, none of us knew what was wrong or what had happened ... We all jumped up and the others all turned back and gathered round the lad on the floor ... Who now had started shaking all over ... Talk about being scared, phewee ...

I was well pooing a brick when this lovely young lady in a nurse's outfit came from some bushes to our right ... Which were the bushes that went round her garden ...

She shouted at us to all stand back then shouted, "Ernie! ... Ernie! I need some help quick!"... Then this young man in a white string vest came over ...

And straight away he seemed to know what the problem was and told the young lady to sit him up ... "C'mon, hurry, sit him up." ... Then he said, "Pass me that bottle."... Which she did ... He gave the lad a drink of this white stuff and straight away he was ok again ...

We all stood back in amazement and said, "How did you fix him so quick?" ... He simply sang out, ... "I'm Ernie the fastest milkman in a vest?" ... Ha ha ha.. That bloomin' Benny Hill, he gets everywhere, what a star eh folks? ...

And us Giddy up gang are still having fun to this day ... When we get together ... Just like the old days ... Yippee ki yeh! ....

Catch you all in the next one ...

29

<u>Some sounds lost to the annals of time</u>

Some old memories to share with you that I'm sure you'll remember too ....

That beautiful sound of children playing and the loud sound of their laughter carried on the breeze ...

And that sound we would hear at night while laying in our beds, the sound of a piano playing in the local pub from down the end of our street with all the patrons in the pub singing along to the tunes played ....

What about the sound of one of our old pals calling us, shouting, "All in ... all in ... captains calling!" .. Bet you're remembering now eh? ....

The sound of the local factory horns tooting at the end of each days shift, what memories eh? ....

The local church bells ringing every Sunday and a lot of Saturdays when there was a wedding taking place ...

The sound of the rag and bone man blowing his horn

and shouting, ... "Rag bone, rag bone .. pots for rags." ... And the sound of his horse's hooves on the cobblestone roads ... Then there was the sound clipperty clop clipperty clop ...

What about the sound of the ringing bells from the fire engines, the ambulances and the police cars? ... Oh boy! .....

The sound of housewives scrubbing and donkey stoning their steps ....

And the thundering sounds of the old steam trains rolling by and their whistles ...

One more is the sound of our Dad's old Big Ben alarm clock waking him up for work ... but it woke the rest of the house up too ..

Or the knocker up man with his long stick tapping on the bedroom window ....

You don't hear these sounds very often these days ... Miss them so much don't you? ....

I'll bet you can think of lots more of the other sounds we've lost from our bygone days as kids too.